BECOMING A PROPHETIC COMMUNITY

J. Elliott Corbett
and
Elizabeth S. Smith

John Knox Press
ATLANTA

All Scripture quotations accompanied by book, chapter, and verse reference alone, and the italic portions of "Appendix: A Modern Paraphrase of the Letter of James (A Prophet of Action)," are from the Revised Standard Version of the Holy Bible, copyright 1946, 1952 and © 1971, 1973 by the Division of Christian Education of the National Council of the Churches of Christ in the U.S.A., and are used by permission.

All Scripture quotations followed by the letters "KJV" are from the King James Version of the Holy Bible.

All unmarked Scripture quotations are paraphrases by the authors.

Library of Congress Cataloging in Publication Data

Corbett, Jack Elliott, 1920-
Becoming a prophetic community.

1. Mission of the church. 2. Prophecy (Christianity)
I. Smith, Elizabeth S., joint author. II. Title.
BV601.8.C67   261.8   80-17618
ISBN 0-8042-0784-4

© copyright John Knox Press 1980
10 9 8 7 6 5 4 3 2 1
Printed in the United States of America
John Knox Press
Atlanta, Georgia

Becoming a Prophetic Community

*Dedicated to
Stephen Elliott Corbett
and
S. Raymond Smith*

ACKNOWLEDGMENTS

The projects described in the text and directory of this book are about people, churches, and religious groups relating their faith to community needs in creative ways. They have been our inspiration. To each we extend our personal thanks.

Surveys for *Becoming a Prophetic Community* were conducted over a two-year period and brought hundreds of replies. To all who responded with a description of a project or directed us to specific programs, we offer our deep appreciation. A special thanks to the many councils of churches and interfaith groups that helped us assemble social action projects. Our only regret is that we were unable to use all the material sent us.

A final note of appreciation is reserved for Richard Ray, Paul Schumacher, and Eva Stimson, editors of John Knox Press, who encouraged us substantially along the way and helpfully improved our manuscript.

J. Elliott Corbett
Elizabeth S. Smith

CONTENTS

Part One

Introduction 13

1. Every Church a Prophetic Community 17
2. The Nature of the Prophetic Task 23
3. How the Prophetic Community Decides 29
4. Fulfilling the Prophetic Function 41
5. The Prophetic Community and Social and Economic Affairs 45
6. The Prophetic Community and Political Affairs 63
7. The Prophetic Community and International Affairs 75

Part Two
Various Models for the Prophetic Community 99

Adult and Senior Citizen Program 102
Advocacy Programs 116
Children's Programs 124
Criminal Justice/Prison Ministries 130
Disaster Relief Programs 135
Education/Information Programs 139
Health and Counseling Programs 146
Housing Programs 154
Hunger Programs 162
Multiservice Programs 168
Peace Programs 178
Rural Programs 182
Youth Programs 190

Appendix:
A Modern Paraphrase of the Letter of James
a Prophet of Action

Notes 199

PART ONE

INTRODUCTION

All prophets in all ages have been warned that they were "destroying society." But actually it has been the prophets who have *kept* society from pushing the self-destruct button. Except when oracles have bounced off of blank walls, the prophets' initiatives have assured society's social salvation.

The world needs the voice and the act of the prophet. Its self-destructive impulse works so silently—like rotting teeth, like termites eating away an old house, like carcinogenic prejudice, like a slowly escalating arms race in which participants are trapped by their self-fulfilling prophecies.

One ancient prophet wrote: "Where there is no vision, the people perish." (Prov. 29:18, KJV) And so it has been throughout the ages.

Moses, the lawgiver, told his people that they would destroy themselves if they remained as brickmakers and hod carriers for the Egyptians. They listened and followed him into the desert and eventually, under other leadership, into the promised land of their salvation.

When in the eighth century B.C. the Hebrew people were confronted by the Assyrian adversary and in danger of utter obliteration, Isaiah denounced leaders of Judah who "go down to Egypt for help" and who "trust in chariots." Instead, shouldn't they "look to the Holy One of Israel" and "consult the LORD"? (Isa. 31:1) King Hezekiah accepted Isaiah's counsel and Judah was spared.

Second Isaiah, the prophet of the exile, taught the followers of Yahweh in an alien land that *their* God was universal; in fact, he was the only God in existence (Isa. 46:9). It was this kind of faith in adopting, at least for a time, the Suffering Servant role—being "a light to the nations" (42:6)—that enabled the little band of aliens to survive and eventually return to Judah.

Jesus of Nazareth, a prophet, though more than a prophet, was an advocate of peaceful change—one who blessed peacemakers, told us to turn the other cheek, and to love our enemies. When defended by a disciple's sword in Gethsemane, he said: "Put your sword back . . . for all who take the sword will perish by the sword." (Matt. 26:52) Jesus was crucified on a cross, his words falling on resistant ground. But a remnant of his followers survived to serve as leaven for a new civilization. Yet the Zealots, who preached violent overthrow in Jesus' day, and who later revolted against the Romans, were utterly destroyed, and all of Jerusalem with them (A.D. 70).

Francis of Assisi, who never became a priest, formed a new order devoted to poverty, humility, and service. He begged for the poor, talked to the birds of the air, and worshiped so intensely that at times his hands and feet bled with the holy stigmata. And thus the gentle friar, who mixed ashes with his food to reject the things of the flesh, was able, through his movement within the church, to save that institution from the ashes of its own destruction.

John Wycliffe, British philosopher of the fourteenth century, attacked the luxurious and corrupt orders of monks. Though a prominent Latin scholar, he felt that the Scriptures should be rendered in the common tongue and he translated them into English accordingly. Feeling that ultimate authority lay in the Scripture, he said: "If there were one hundred popes, and all the friars were turned into cardinals, their opinion ought not to be acceded to in matters of faith *except* in so far as they base themselves on Scripture."[1] Wycliffe was declared a heretic 44 years after his death and his bones were removed from consecrated ground, burned and the ashes thrown in the Severn River. Yet his translation survived to exert a significant influence on the King James Version.

Roger Williams founded Rhode Island in seventeenth-century America as a refuge from religious intolerance. He was the first to organize and build up a political community founded upon absolute religious liberty. Roger Williams was constantly harassed by the New England Confederacy and endured open hostility from the Massachusetts Bay Colony. When Quakers were persecuted in Boston, they were made welcome in Rhode Island. In stressing the ideal of a free church in a free state, Roger Williams saved America from the scourge of religious bigotry.

John Woolman, Quaker tailor from Mount Holly, New Jersey, devoted much of his life to opposing slavery about a century before the Abolitionist movement took hold in the New World. So concerned was Woolman over the slavery issue that, after he heard that the dyes of the West Indies were prepared through the use of slave labor, he thenceforth wore suits of white, undyed material. Thus, he made his witness against an unconscionable institution. Once, when captured by his opponents, he was cast into a pit and refuse was thrown down on his head. Yet it was Woolman's insight and witness that helped initiate a movement that eventually saved America from continuing a thoroughly inhumane practice.

John Wesley, through his evangelical and social reform movement in eighteenth-century England, may have saved his nation from utter corruption and deterioration. Before Wesley's missional efforts, it was difficult to convene a quorum of sober members of Parliament. The prisons were filthy and persons were cast behind bars for minor debts. So insensitive was the populace that criminals were publicly hanged for a price of admission. The Wesleyan movement cleaned up the prisons, launched the public education system, initiated health clinics in the slums, and provided the moral force for spearheading the antislavery drive.

And in our own day, Martin Luther King, Jr. emerged into public view about the time racial tensions were beginning to tear apart the fabric of the nation. He "walked for freedom," leading his people in a nonviolent struggle for their civil rights. Many persons hated him and spit at him and threw rocks at him because he asserted his right to be human. Even J. Edgar Hoover of the F.B.I. attempted to blaspheme his witness. But through his preaching of nonviolence and returning good for evil, blessing for cursing, he earned the right to leadership and respect. And as he became a "suffering servant," by his wounds we were all healed, healed of our innate prejudice, healed of our superior pride.

§

So the prophetic witness has been made through the years, a witness in words that have often been unpleasant and unwelcome and in deeds that have embarrassed humankind in its callous guilt.

The prophets were able to articulate a collective discontent. But this was not their primary mission. For they were to be spokespersons for God—to speak forth "the hard sayings" that society needed to hear but would resist. We would be told that they were "destroying the nation," but of a truth history would prove that they were in fact "saving the nation."

What are some of the "hard sayings" that need to be heard today?

- —That, despite mounting drunken driving fatalities, an increasing number of persons are served liquor in establishments adjacent to highways and are drunk when they leave to reenter the traffic lanes.
- —That it will be impossible to integrate our public education system in any normal fashion until we find a way to establish interracial housing in neighborhoods and communities.
- —That defense expenditures—spending for nonconsumable goods—are a major inflationary factor in the U.S. economy.
- —That millions of children of working mothers receive inadequate day care—some get no more than orange juice, graham crackers, and television—and drastic action must be taken to remedy it.
- —That the United States, the breadbasket of the world, must not use its

grain supplies as a weapon to force starving and malnourished nations to conform to its foreign policy whims (sit up and beg for crumbs).
— That as long as churches invest their surplus funds in weapons manufacturers, violaters of fair employment, exploiters of labor, and polluters of the earth, air, and water, then the public will not take seriously the church's pronouncements on peace, race, work, and "stewardship of resources."
— That in the long run we really need to live in an interdependent world whatever short-run advantages there may be to "energy independence."
— That we must stop using foreign aid to shore up military dictatorships so as to "stabilize" society and make American overseas investments safe.
— That increasing our weapons stocks as "bargaining chips" is the same tired argument as needing "arms to parlay" which never succeeded in halting the arms race but escalated it.

§

Today the prophetic community must assume a role as heir to the prophetic witness. It is a community which normally will take shape within the church. But the church has no monopoly on conscience. Such a prophetic community has a special function to witness, educate, serve, and act in the name of God and his compassion. Especially to act. If they do so, they will be sharply criticized. But, nevertheless, they will be the backfire, the thumb in the dike, the builder that outstrips the destroyer, the war vaccinator, the grain-producing desert, indeed, the redemptive force for peaceful change in our society. And they shall fulfill the promise of Christ's coming long ago— "For God sent the Son into the world, not to condemn the world, but that the world might be *saved* through him." (John 3:17, emphasis added)

Unashamedly, the prophetic community accepts the deprecating epithet society would bestow upon it—"World-saver."

§

In the pages that follow, J. Elliott Corbett has written Part One and "Appendix: A Modern Paraphrase of the Letter of James," while Elizabeth S. Smith assembled and wrote the "Various Models for the Prophetic Community."

1.
EVERY CHURCH A PROPHETIC COMMUNITY

Every church should be a prophetic community. Otherwise it is not fulfilling its appointed mission in society.

That is not to say it is not good for the church to study, to worship, or to give to missions. But for the church to fulfill its historically assigned prophetic task, the church must be a "doing church." Its members must be personally and corporately engaged in some kind of service and/or action which relates to improving the lives of human beings.

Some have said the business of the church is to develop attitudes. But attitudes which have strength and depth are best developed when a person has a chance to test them out in a real life situation. One can be in a study group and come to the conclusion that providing clothing for overseas relief is needed. But until one engages in a clothing-collection project—like working for a day at the Church World Service clothing center at New Windsor, Maryland—such an attitude may not represent a solid commitment.

A study group in a church may give attention to the area of penal reform. But until the class visits the county jail or state penitentiary or becomes involved in work with those on probation and parole, its ideas may lack sufficient experiential base.

One church may study the problems of the aging. Another may initiate a "meals on wheels" program and become acquainted with situations faced by the aging firsthand. One church may discuss the question of gun control; another may send a delegation to sit in the emergency room of a large city hospital to observe the cases of firearms assault as they come staggering in or are carried bleeding on a stretcher during one hot summer weekend. One church group may read a book on "juvenile delinquency"; another may spend several frustrating days witnessing what goes on in a juvenile court.

Up-Against-the-Wall Christianity

What is really needed in the churches is an "up-against-the-wall" Christianity. Only when Christians are sufficiently pressed back upon their resources will study be meaningful, worship needful, and action obviously imperative. The church that puts its members in difficult and traumatic situations will be:

- —the church whose people realize their ignorance and want to study more about the problem;
- —the church that must call upon God to help them because their own resources are insufficient;
- —the church that is moved to act because it sees the problem more clearly and is emotionally motivated to engage in at least a modest related project.

Problems in this world are not as simple as they appear on the printed page. Even giving someone "a cup of cold water" in kindness may be hedged about with reservations: Is there fluoride in the water? What is the level of carcinogenic chlorine? Has the water been tested for purity?

Study is important for the Christian. Yet it is generally meaningless when divorced from related action. As a matter of fact, it may even be a crime to read this book if it means that church members—after they have finished discussing it—will dust off their hands and turn to other innocent non-involvements.

Hardly any congregation could be called a "church" if there were no worship. But that, in some instances, is all a church may do. Pity the poor small country church which, as part of a circuit, can just barely get a seminary student to come out once a week and practice preaching on them.

Beyond a period of worship which helps define the existence of a church (it's not a church anymore if there aren't services), some churches do manage an active social life. And thus the fellowship is built. The next normal building block in church development is a study program. This may be a church school, youth meeting, or special classes for adults, etc.

From that point on, in the United States, most churches have been stunted in their religious development. They remain spiritual dwarfs. Oh, they may raise some money for missions, but as far as the members themselves being involved in Christian action projects, nothing doing. But where Christians *are* so involved, the tone of the whole congregation is different.

The Action Church

There are several ways that the *action church* may express itself—through social witness, social service, and social change.

Social witness means that a group of Christians will engage in a corporate act which reflects their faith and their convictions. It might be so simple a thing as singing Christmas carols at the County Home. Or better yet, the choir singing at that home on a nonholiday in the Christian calendar. It might mean a group of church people going to a public trial or a hearing and expressing by their presence concern that justice be done.

By *social service,* I mean service to the community—outside of the church. If a church prepares a meal for students at a nearby seminary because their cafeteria is shut down for the weekend, this is certainly a good thing. But it is not social service; it is the church acting on behalf of its own (future ministers).

Social service might be a delegation visiting a home for the aged and reading to residents who no longer can read. (They will go wild over Lawrence Welk's *Wunnerful, Wunnerful!*) It may be collecting useful garage-sale type furniture and taking it to Goodwill Industries. It could be a group of laypersons who decide to take training and serve as voluntary probation officers for the juvenile court.

Or it may be trying to relate to the problem of insufficient low- and moderate-income housing. There is a shortage of at least five or six million housing units in the United States. Yet there are over 300,000 churches in America. What if every church decided to rehabilitate *one* house and make it livable? If a family of five were to occupy such a dwelling, and every church in the nation did this, that would mean providing housing for a million and a half persons!

What this means practically is starting out with a house that is basically sound in its foundation and structure but still needs a lot of work on it. Some of the floors need replacing. New siding may be required. A new roof may have to be installed. Faulty electric wiring and plumbing may need replacing. When you're all through, a couple of coats of paint might make it look spanking new.

But what do we do for money? A modest amount of basic seed money would be needed. But church groups should be able to secure a rehabilitation loan through the new Housing and Community Development Act. You could check with the city or county about such funds being available. A 40-year mortgage could be set up; and a family moving in, after proper screening, could pay less than they would for rent anywhere else. Such a project would truly be providing social service for the community.

When we turn to *social change* we are in a different element entirely. Social change means engaging in an activity which gets at the root of the problem. It is much more difficult, for it means dealing with causes rather than results. Only the more adventurous churches will try this. But it is intriguing. It means changing the system or the way the system operates.

For instance, if a church knows that the county judge is involved in a racket to get unwed pregnant girls to sell their babies for $10,000 apiece, social change may mean running an honorable person against the judge in the next election instead of just setting up a home to take care of unwed mothers, commendable as that may be.

A group in the church may be investigating housing needs of low-income people. They may discover that the people who live across the tracks or across the river are living in substandard dwellings, where there are no adequate foundations and the winter wind whips up into the houses through cracks in the floorboards. To get action they may have to appear as a body before the next meeting of the county zoning board and ask for a more rigorous housing code. If they don't get action, someone on the committee may have to get "soiled hands" and run for office.

One group may be working in the church to publicize the fact that the county's poor are entitled to food stamps. That would be service. But if the group determines to see that the county welfare agency changes its policies and undertakes the job of itself publicizing the availability of food stamps, that would be promoting social change.

Many laypersons engage in money-raising projects for the church. They do this so that funds can be provided to enable others to engage in mission. Those who are engaged on the church's behalf may be missionaries; they may work in the slums; they may facilitate low- and moderate-income housing; they may work for the interests of Native Americans; they may relate to the needs of migrant workers; they may be involved in international development projects, etc., etc.

But the question is: Why don't the people of the church spend less time raising money so others can go for them in the mission of the church, and why don't they use more of their time directly carrying on the mission of the church themselves?

Why let the church bureaucrats have all the fun?

§

In this volume there will be an attempt to lay the theoretical groundwork for laypersons developing an "action church." Also, in Part Two of the book there is a listing of church-sponsored and -supported projects which have been successful in various local communities around the country.

These could serve as models for projects undertaken by your own church. An address is given for interested parties to write for further information. You may send a modest amount along to help cover costs, as indicated.

Let the church be an experience of religious inspiration for its participants. Let it also be an encounter with enlightenment. But beyond that, let the church be an opportunity for active involvement in "doing Christianity." Let the church become a prophetic community.

2.

THE NATURE OF THE PROPHETIC TASK

The great prophets of the Old Testament lived in the eighth and sixth centuries B.C. The eighth and sixth centuries were times of tremendous turbulence for the Hebrew people, years which preceded the deadly destruction of the Northern and Southern Kingdoms. Generally speaking, the prophets were *forth-tellers,* not fore-tellers. They spoke about the future in only the most general terms: if Israel lived close to God and obeyed his commands, the nation would live and prosper; but if the Hebrew people turned to false gods and rejected the will of the God of Abraham, they would be utterly destroyed.

On the other hand, the prophets delivered their prophetic utterances in very specific terms. They spoke about

> selling the needy for a
>   pair of sandals
> and dealing deceitfully
>   with false scales;
> daughters playing the harlot
>   and men kissing calves;
> coveting fields and seizing them
>   and houses and taking them away.

Dealing with the Specific

The church is fulfilling its prophetic mission only when *it is dealing with the specific:* for instance, when it is

- —protesting escalating arms expenditures;
- —calling for busing wherever attending neighborhood schools means perpetuating segregated schools;
- —questioning the real-estate tax as an appropriate base for providing equal education;
- —calling for the kind of developmental child care enabling women on welfare to work outside the home if that's their choice, instead of blaming them for lack of supervision of their children.

Speaking Truth to Power

Second, a church is in prophetic mission *when truth is spoken to power.* The prophets were political advisors to the kings of Israel and Judah. It was as natural and common for Isaiah to pay a visit to King Ahaz as it was for Billy Graham to see Mr. Nixon. However, the comparison stops there. For the major prophets of Hebrew history made a sharp distinction between the true prophets and the false prophets. The true prophet—who was subsequently canonized—occasionally had a few comforting words for the king. More often his encounter was advisory and frequently critical. Perhaps the strangest aspect of the prophet-king encounter was (1) that the prophet appeared unannounced, and (2) that given his likely message, they let him in the palace at all.

In the case of Amos, the priest Amaziah did not complain to the king that the prophet uttered untruths. He said "the land is not able to bear all his words." (7:10) In effect, Amaziah told Amos to go back home to Judah where he belonged. "Prophesy there," he said, "but never again prophesy at Bethel." (7:12) He told Amos that his prophecies were an embarrassment to the elite at Bethel for "it is the king's sanctuary." (7:13)

The false prophets were a different breed. Their sycophantish stance caused no embarrassment at the palace. They told the king what he wanted to hear. Though they were popular in their own day, recorded history generally ignores their names.

Speaking truth to power is no simple task for the religionist in the current age. Those religious leaders who surrounded President Nixon in the Vietnam War period, for instance, were not prone to displease him. Other religious leaders—those representing the major church bodies—did not even have entrée to the president's hearing.

During that tumultuous era, syndicated columnist Clayton Fritchey stated:

In all the years Billy Graham has been unofficial chaplain to the White House, he has never criticized the war policy of either Lyndon Johnson or Richard Nixon. Listed not long ago by George Gallup as the second most popular American, Mr. Graham recently issued a statement defending his position on the Vietnam war. He said: "I have spoken and continue to speak on issues in which I feel a definite moral issue is involved." But he never did say anything about the recent bombing of Hanoi, despite urging by ten prominent religious leaders. This restraint is apparently explained in his own statement where he says: "I am convinced that God has called me to be a New Testament evangelist, not an Old Testament prophet!" This fairly well clarifies his own role as well as the role he assigns to the prophet from Nazareth.[2]

The prophetic community may experience great difficulty in effectively speaking truth to power. I recall Bishop James Armstrong, perhaps the major "peace bishop" of United Methodism, expressing his frustration at the response he received to a wire he sent to the White House opposing the bombing of Haiphong and Hanoi. The answer came back: "Dear Bishop Armstrong, We greatly appreciate your support of the President in this time of national crisis," etc., etc.

During the December 1972 bombing of Hanoi, Henry Niles, president of an insurance company and head of Business Executives Move for Peace in Vietnam, phoned the White House to protest this new war initiative. When he expressed his purpose in calling, an official said: "I'm sorry. We are not taking any messages just now regarding the war." A few hours later, Mr. Niles's wife—an enterprising Quaker woman—also called the White House to test out the machinery. She inquired of an official if she could leave a message for the president *in support of* the administration's bombing policy. The official replied: "Oh, yes. We'll put you on record right away. You have 60 seconds to present your message."

Despite all the obstacles placed in the path of the prophetic community, our task is still clear: we must seek in every way possible to speak truth to power. This means we must write the letters to public officials, send the public opinion messages for $2.50, make the telephone calls. It means preparing testimony for the city council hearings; it means seeing one's representative in congress when he or she is in the home district. Particularly, on national issues, it means relating to the congress—for I foresee in the years ahead stronger attempts on the part of the legislative branch to reassert its authority vis-à-vis the executive. We are able to strengthen their hand in this effort.

Proposing Specific Alternatives

Also, the prophetic task is being performed when *specific alternatives are being proposed.*

When Amos objected to the Israelites becoming involved in the machinations of meaningless ritual, it is true that he said: "let justice roll down like waters, and righteousness like an everflowing stream." (5:24)

He wasn't content, however, to leave such terms as "justice" and "righteousness" to congenial generality. He was specific. And so he proposed that his hearers engage in honest business practices, treat slaves as human beings, show concern for the poor, rebuild cities, and plant gardens.

Jeremiah also spoke in general terms, saying: "Amend your ways and your doings" but then went on to say: "for if you truly . . . execute justice one with another, if you do not oppress the alien, the fatherless or the widow, or shed innocent blood in this place, and if you do not go after other gods to your own hurt, then I will let you dwell in this place, in the land that I gave of old to your fathers for ever." (7:5-7)

It is true that Isaiah generalized, saying: "Woe to those who call evil good and good evil." (5:20)

But he also particularized, following this by proclaiming:

> Woe to those who are heroes at drinking wine,
>   and valiant men in mixing strong drink,
> who acquit the guilty for a bribe,
>   and deprive the innocent of his right! [5:22-23]

And thus today the prophetic task calls the church to set forth specific alternatives to the evils we deplore. Complaint, though the essence of democracy, is not enough.

It is a sobering thought indeed that during the period of our involvement in the Vietnam War, more American citizens were killed in automobile accidents involving alcohol use than were killed in the Southeast Asian conflict. Traditionally the church has dealt with the problem of alcohol by supporting prohibition, opposing liquor by the drink, and urging rehabilitation programs. And yet I am confident that if the church ever rallied its forces behind a concrete proposal to effectively meet the problem of drunken driving, it could rack up a trophy.

The problem of busing continues to aggravate American communities. The general opposition cry is, "We want to preserve the neighborhood school." No one will argue that there are not considerable values in the preservation of such schools. But the real question for us would be: What kind of an alternative proposal could we come up with which would preserve the neighborhood school, integrate the neighborhoods, and keep busing to a minimum? A prophetic community should be giving a lot of thought to some such longer-range solution, rather than to allow the dialogue to simply center on the mechanism of "the yellow submarine."

When the Corporate Information Center of the National Council of

Churches published its report on church investments in January of 1972 in the *New York Times,* it caused considerable consternation in United Methodist quarters because that church stood at the top of the list in terms of investments in companies with military contracts. The church had almost $60 million in such companies. One of the major offenders was the Methodist Ministers Pension Fund with assets totaling $417 million. They had substantial investments in firms manufacturing antipersonnel bombs, atomic missiles, M-16 rifles, tanks, products for automated air war, etc.

When the Pension Board office was contacted as early as 1968 urging them to divest their war stocks, they dug their heels in the carpet. The stock answer was: "We have to produce earnings for our retiring preachers." One can just picture retired United Methodist preachers basking in the Florida sunshine with the comforting assurance that all this has been made possible through the courtesy of Honeywell, United Aircraft, and I.T.T.! After hearing this "can't be done" answer from a number of church agencies, certain church leaders made a conscious decision to demonstrate that there could be a viable alternate policy. So an intermediary institution (called Pax World Fund) was set up which would invest only in peace stocks—such as food, building materials, hospital supplies, education, pollution control, etc. At the same time the institution would seek a normal return.

After having the chance to review the Pension Board's portfolio recently, I am glad to report that they have now unloaded a large proportion of their war stocks. They are still receiving a reasonable return. I honestly believe that two factors were determinative in their taking this action: (1) they were embarrassed by adverse publicity (the speaking of truth to ecclesiastical power) and (2) an alternative investment channel existed which demonstrated that it was possible to focus on life-supportive goods and services.

Seeking Social Change

Fourth, the church is being a prophetic community when it is attempting to *alter fundamental social policies.* This means moving beyond social witness and social service to seeking *social change.*

Amos certainly was seeking a basic change in the social system that had mired the people of Israel in meaningless ritual and insensitive luxury.

Isaiah warned the kings of Judah against the kind of international system which had enmeshed the Jewish state in destructive entangling alliances.

Second Isaiah, among the Babylonian exiles, championed the kind of universal religion that enabled Judaism, formerly Temple-oriented, to live creatively anywhere on the earth.

These were fundamental changes. They weren't simply patching up something that hadn't worked well before, or picking away at the fringes of a system wrongheaded at the core.

Therefore, we must say that a truly prophetic community today would seek basic and radical reform under which our social systems would be substantially altered. I do not use the word "revolution"—which too many people toss around as though it were a harmless firecracker. I do not see the need generally for our society to make a 180-degree turn. It is more like a ninety-degree turn, a turn toward compassion, justice, and peace.

Thus, the church is being a prophetic community when it:

— goes beyond setting up day-care centers on its premises and works for developmental child care as an instrument of national policy;
— supports the kind of tax reform which not only looks at oil depletion allowances and accelerating depreciation, but at church benefits such as tax-free parsonages and clergy housing allowances;
— not only opposes war but examines closely a whole social system which makes American society violence-prone;
— is not only working to ameliorate the inequities of the welfare program, but actively supporting the institution of a basic income-maintenance system for the poor;
— is not only holding seminars at the Church Center for the United Nations but is actively pushing for the proposal to turn seven-tenths of the globe—namely the oceans—over to the United Nations' authority.

§

To summarize, the church is fulfilling its prophetic function when it is spotlighting injustices in our society, speaking truth to power, proposing specific alternatives, and attempting to alter basic social policy.

3.

HOW THE PROPHETIC COMMUNITY DECIDES

Many Christians never accomplish very much in terms of results because they can't make up their minds. Of course, it is never easy to make up one's mind, but there is an orderly way of going about it. Undoubtedly a lot of Christians never rely upon a system or a procedure in their decision-making; they make up their minds as a matter of course simply depending upon their "gut feeling."

But one doesn't have to do this. There are a number of logical, methodical ways of making up one's mind when faced with a particular problem.

Applying Christian Principles

One of these ways is to simply apply Christian principles. Apply truth. Apply love. Apply mercy. If there is some confusion over what one is to do, then find out the facts. Look into the research. Be guided by knowledge which can shed light on a solution. For instance, if one is dealing with a question as involved as the Watergate affair, then getting out the facts is very important. And that's why the Senate Watergate Committee held hearings on this important subject.

Or, on the other hand, perhaps one wonders what to do about food shortages and starvation in the sub-Sahara region. There were conflicting accounts being published about this. What does the Food and Agriculture Organization say? How about the Agency for International Development? the Peace Corps? on-the-scene observers? If the need really does not exist, then that would tend to negate action at all. If the need is focused in certain areas, that would call for a particularized response. If the need is desperate and general throughout the area, then an all-out and broadly dispersed thrust would seem to be the answer.

Or take another situation where a church, with a substantial endowment and a prestigious reputation, now finds itself in an area of the city where some of the housing is deteriorating badly. In several blocks nearby the church, persons with pride and a sense of responsibility are trying to keep their homes up. But four or five of the deteriorating row houses in their block are going downhill. They have been purchased by the city housing authority for rehabilitation but funds are not available to fix them up. Their windows are broken. Doors hang off the hinges. Bricks are falling away from crumbling mortar. Transients are using the vacant buildings to sleep in and addicts for a shooting gallery. Remaining residents on the block are fearful for their children in this environment. If they wanted to sell their property, who would want to buy?

For the church in this neighborhood what does love mean? How can the principle be applied? What can the church do to keep these houses from deteriorating? Can anything be done to rally the financial resources of the government and/or financial institutions to get some rehabilitation projects moving? How can the Christian community express loving concern for the derelicts—and addicts? If a holding action is necessary, what could the church people do to close off the vacated housing so that it will be fit for renewal when funds become available? There are many ways that the principle of love can be applied.

The Empirical Approach

Another valid approach to decision-making is experientially based. One considers his/her experience in business, government, the university, the church, and based on this makes a value judgment concerning an ethical question. This is, without doubt, an *inductive* approach to ethics. Why shouldn't one use the wisdom that God, out of his goodness, has given us through the means of our experience?

Here is a secretary who is working for a nonprofit agency. She is an alien. In her own culture she has earned the master's degree in literature. But in English she has trouble with the meaning, spelling, and pronunciation of words. Thus, it becomes necessary for her employer, with regret, to let her go. How does he break the news? Of course, since he likes the woman personally, he procrastinates. He knows that she may be out of a job for a while. He also knows she has talent. Further, he realizes that she has rights and, as a foreign-born person, will elicit sympathy from her fellow employees if he dismisses her without apparent cause. His experience comes to his rescue as he realizes that the basic problem is that she is overtrained for a job which primarily requires excellent typing.

Thus, the executive levels with the secretary and tells her that she doesn't quite fit into this slot and that she should be doing other work at a higher level. He has discussed the matter with the personnel manager and they have agreed it would be a disservice to the secretary to maintain her in this type of job. No jobs are open in the organization commensurate with her particular talents—editing, etc. They have decided to give her a month to look for other employment in keeping with her capabilities. She finds a better job and quits.

In this instance, if the employer had been inexperienced, he might have muddled the case. He could have caused the organization grave difficulty, a rift among his employees, and unhappiness and loss of dignity on the part of the secretary. But he had seen somewhat similar situations before, and his experience led him to handle this one with aptness and reasonable compassion.

The Universal Approach

Under the universal approach a person emphasizes the oneness and universality of God as II Isaiah did in Isaiah 43:10: "Before me no god was formed, nor shall there be any after me." Also, Christ stressed *"Our Father"* and related with equal concern to Roman, Jew, Greek, Samaritan, and Syrophoenician.

Such a universal approach rules out ingroup and outgroup morality. That ethical standard was reflected well in Deuteronomy 23:20: "To a foreigner you may lend upon interest, but to your brother you shall not lend upon interest." Usury was outlawed within the Hebrew community. But it was all right to make money through interest by lending to the outgroup, the foreigner. Another example of this standard may be found in Deuteronomy 14:21: "You shall not eat anything that dies of itself; you may give it to the alien who is within your towns, that he may eat it, or you may sell it to a foreigner." So if an animal died a natural death, you could sell the carcass to a foreigner, but must not attempt to sell it to a fellow Jew.

In American community life the ingroup morality ethic is most easily seen in the treatment one is supposed to accord to one's lodge brothers. He is supposed to give them preferential treatment in social life and business transactions. In no way is he to take advantage of them or their families. (In one prominent American lodge, members promise never to commit adultery with daughters of brother lodge members.) No such special behavior is required in relationships with non-lodgemembers.

It is difficult, of course, to be objective enough to treat the outgroup with equal consideration and compassion. For instance, a Gallup poll taken at the conclusion of the Vietnam War showed that only 40% of the American people believed the United States should help rebuild North Vietnam. At the same time, the vast majority of Americans believed that substantial reconstruction aid should be extended to South Vietnam.

If one uses a universal approach, one must apply the same ethical principles equally to all peoples. For a universal God loves all people equally. Thus, Russians are to be loved as well as Americans, blacks as well as whites (if one is white), Arabs as well as Jews (even though one's neighbors may be Jewish), atheists as well as Christians. This does not mean that certain individual people are not loved more than others simply because of the kind of people they are. Rather, it means that they are not loved more simply because of their race or national origin. Serious Christians, embracing this approach, will try to make their love as impartial as they know God's love to be.

Situation Ethics

Dr. Joseph Fletcher has challenged the old more simplified method of applying Christian principles. He suggests situation ethics. The old principles are not helpful and do not apply. The situation we face is a new one and must be faced existentially. In this system, love is the only norm. He defines love as that which "wills the neighbor's good." Further, he states that *"love and justice are the same, for justice is love distributed."* [3]

The world is always turning up new situations, true enough. For example, we used to think that a doctor's job was to keep the patient alive as long as possible. However, with advances in medical technology, it is often possible for hospitals to keep a patient's heart going almost indefinitely through artificial means, even after the patient's brain has lost its power to function. In this situation, what is the doctor's role; what does love prescribe? Is there any way that "the neighbor's good" is being advanced if the patient's life is merely prolonged in vegetable existence?

Dr. Fletcher tends to use rather bizarre examples in demonstrating that Christian principles can't always be rigorously applied. He tells of the woman interned in a Nazi war prisoner's camp who used sex as a means to escape to freedom. Which was more important, her life or rigid adherence to the seventh commandment?

It is true that new situations are always emerging which seem to defy any strict use of traditional norms. Yet it is also true that, in this brand of ethics, one is tempted to justify each situation as being new and unique and therefore outside the help of history, that is, outside the application of Christian principles. Also, one is in danger of interpreting "love" selfishly and thus ending up doing as one pleases.

Yet we do know that there are extenuating circumstances and that, in the face of an increasingly complex world, it is ever more difficult to apply "the simple gospel."

Time Preference

One base for an ethical system is rooted in one's willingness to make a present sacrifice to obtain a future good. In economics this is called "time preference." Yet it equally applies to religious norms.

In a family this is often illustrated by parents' willingness to forgo their own pleasures (travel, etc.) in order that they may contribute substantially to their children's college education.

In our nation today it could mean the willingness of citizens to drive at 55 miles an hour or less and turn their thermostats down to 65 degrees in winter if this holds the promise of providing for the basic energy needs of our society now and for the future.

Or, in the United States, it could well mean the acceptance by business and society of price and wage controls if this was understood as a temporary means used to curb inflation.

Or again, time preference could be implemented by young couples who limit their families to two children in order to set the example on behalf of a less crowded planet in the future.

For the person who gives consideration to time preference, the moment of truth is not *now* but in the future.

Approaching the Limits

"Approaching the limits" is a calculus term which in mathematics means that, in working out a problem, one can achieve not that which is an absolute definitive solution but a working answer. When we rely upon this method, we attempt to find a working hypothesis somewhere between the absolute ethic and the relative ethic. We "approach the limits" of the absolute, but do not arrive there. Though we are well aware of what the absolute ethic is, we do not obtain it but instead find a working ethical solution somewhat short of this.

We see this in Jesus' declaring that "The sabbath was made for man, not man for the sabbath." (Mark 2:27) This does not mean that in most instances Jesus would not have observed the Jewish sabbath laws. Undoubtedly he did observe them. Yet when pragmatically he saw certain things that needed to be done on the sabbath out of compassion, he was willing to give the sabbath a shortfall. Thus, one man could be healed on the sabbath and another man could work to the extent of getting his ox out of the ditch on the sabbath.

It is recognized that we cannot base our lives mainly on the exceptions, but must live under the general rules. Thus, we attempt to approach the limits of perfection, but never completely achieve it.

Balancing Principles

Kenneth Thompson of the Rockefeller Foundation has stressed the importance of balancing principles as one makes an ethical decision. One of the illustrations Dr. Thompson often refers to is the utter impracticability of Woodrow Wilson's "open covenants openly arrived at." He calls this "goldfish diplomacy" and says that it is impossible because diplomats cannot surface their tentative proposals and bargaining positions for fear that the constituency of their own nation may come to believe this position represents the *objective* of the negotiators. If caught in this bind, diplomats could never test out their opposite numbers with any potential solutions for fear these might be taken completely seriously back home. Thus, the principle of truth comes in conflict with the principle of reconciliation and peace.[4]

In Vichy, France, many a Jewish neighbor was hidden during the duration of World War II by a friend. If the Nazis or their French police subordinates came to the door, was the friend to lie to the intruders, or out of truth turn the Jew in? Thus, truth and love are often in conflict in a particular situation.

In our own nation we have seen this happen in the case of the Watergate affair. Was it appropriate for the Ervin Committee, Judge Sirica, and Special Prosecutor Archibald Cox to seek out the truth about Watergate wherever it might lead, even to the White House and office of the president, or, out of love for the president and his fine family and lovely daughters, ignore the truth and bypass the investigation?

Lest we fall victim to thinking that every situation is new, perhaps we need to realize that most situations fall into patterns and are unique only in superficial ways. And there is nothing particularly new about principles being in conflict. Jesus himself faced this in healing the man with the withered hand on the sabbath. Two principles were in conflict: strict adherence to the sabbath observance versus compassion for the handicapped man. Jesus chose compassion. But one could not say he didn't apply principles in this difficult situation where his adversaries were anxious to find fault with him. Jesus simply chose one principle as being more important than another.

I recall returning home one Sunday afternoon from an extended field trip and discovering that my grass was about a foot high. Ordinarily I don't like to spend Sunday engaged in manual labor, but that day I determined to get the job done before the lawn became completely unmanageable. My churchy neighbor across the street caught me at the task and I felt a bit sheepish about "working on the Lord's day." But he granted me absolution by hollering across the street: "There are times you have to get your ox out of the ditch!" So suggested Jesus (Luke 14:5), and his balancing of principles brought some reasonableness and sanity into the world.

One is faced with balancing principles all the time. It isn't a question of choosing what is clearly good over what is clearly evil. This is an easy choice and when confronted in that way (which isn't often!) a person should leap to make the choice. Much more often the choice is between the better of two goods or the lesser of two evils. In this particular instance, which is the higher good? Love is not always superior to truth. For example, in some colleges where there is an "honor system," students are taught to tell the truth if a fellow student cheats even though they may like the cheating student.

Sempathy—An Attitudinal Stance

Still another approach might be to determine one's attitude of "sempathy" toward others. This lies somewhere between sympathy on the one hand and empathy on the other. A dictionary definition of sympathy renders the term as "the capacity to enter into the feelings of another." Whereas empathy is defined as "the capacity for participation in another's feelings."

Thus (according to Corbett's Revised Standard Version of the dictionary!), "sempathy" is "the ability to identify oneself adequately with the need or suffering of others and yet remain sufficiently objective so as to render effective aid."

The difference between "sympathy" and "empathy" is basically the degree of identification—sympathetic persons enter into the feelings of others but usually only somewhat; empathetic persons so completely identify themselves that they fully participate in the feelings of others. Emotionally, the empathetic person *becomes* the other person.

Sempathy is then the needful nuance, the shade of meaning which represents a combination of the best elements of both sympathy and empathy. We need to go farther than sympathy in dealing with others, but not as far as empathy.

Perhaps the best model that we have for the *sempathetic* personality is the good Samaritan story. It is quite possible that the priest and the Levite in that story had sympathy for the beaten man. They may even have said:

"Poor fellow! I must report this to the police when I get to Jericho!" Or they may have cared but, like certain urban people today, they may have been afraid to get involved, to identify themselves with this unfortunate victim whose assailants could even now be lurking behind some hillside pass. So they drew their emotional curtains.

But the good Samaritan, Jesus said, "had compassion"—that is, initial sympathy and then enough empathy to identify himself with the stricken Jew so that he forgot his Samaritanness and bound up his wounds. Had sympathy been his primary motivation he might have shed a few tears, or handled the situation with thorough objectivity by sending for some first-century ambulance. Or, had the Samaritan suffered from the affliction of empathy, the man's wounds would have pained him, the sight of blood sickened him, and, fainting, he would have fallen to the ground beside the naked, beaten, half-dead man.

Such persons as doctors, social workers, and ministers particularly need to walk the uneasy line strung between sympathy and empathy.

For example, the sympathetic type of minister may preach funerals with mournful tones, but forget all about the grief-stricken family ten minutes after the service. Or the pastor may speak with passion about the war on poverty from the pulpit, but be adept at referring all destitute people to the Salvation Army headquarters in the next town.

In the case of the empathetic pastor, if any baby being baptized cries, the day is ruined and the consecutive record broken. Every divorce of a couple such a pastor has joined together is a personal blight on the pastor's career. Or again, the empathetic pastor's ulcer may be activated by the groan of each hospital patient.

But how does one apply sempathy to the social scene? One of the places where it has been most difficult for U.S. citizens is in the periodically tense Middle East situation. Those of us who live in the United States encounter our Jewish friends as neighbors and fellow workers, so naturally we are likely to be sympathetic to them. Not all, but most Jewish persons hold a positive indentification with Israel, one that borders on the empathetic. Whenever Israel bleeds, Jews in the United States feel the pain. But the situation is quite different regarding Arab nations. Very few Arabs live in the United States, except in New York in connection with the United Nations community. It is difficult for most of us to move as far on the spectrum as even sympathy when it comes to feeling for the Arab states, let alone being sempathetic toward them. Thus, in a sense, if we are to apply sempathy to the Middle East, we as Christians need to restrain our feelings somewhat toward Israel when we are heavily influenced by an empathetic Jewish community and we need to exert ourselves to understand and identify with Arab nations, even though their cutback on oil shipments causes inconvenience and discomfort to many of us.

How do we as individuals achieve *sempathy?* I do not know. We cannot seek it by going through a process any more than we can successfully seek humility. But we must keep the goal before us as an end and depend upon the grace of God as the means—to make us care, keep us objective, and yet identify enough with a suffering world to be responsible.

The Possible Good

Determining what "the possible good" is is yet another means to socially responsible decision-making. Dr. Harvey Seifert, in a booklet entitled *Decision-Making in World Affairs,* states: "Working for the 'impossible perfect' instead of the 'possible good', simply means donating the victory to whomever is supporting the 'possible bad.' "[5]

Too often Christians have dissipated their energies by devoting their time to those high ideals which were perpetually elusive. For example, while Methodists were zealously working on behalf of prohibition (the impossible perfect), alcoholism and slaughter on the highways increased (the possible bad). It would have been more sensible if similar efforts had been focused on eliminating drunken driving (a possible good).

Through most of the 1960s Christian leaders were concerned about obtaining worldwide total disarmament—the impossible perfect at that time. As a result, the arms race actually accelerated in terms of budgets and sophisticated nuclear weapons. There were certain possible goods which were in the realm of the achievable, such as overseas troop cuts in Europe and the economic conversion of domestic military plants and bases to peaceful purposes. As to the latter, it will always be difficult to get a member of congress to vote to close a military installation in his or her own district with the resulting loss of jobs among constituents. But if these could be converted to peaceful uses—parks, making trucks instead of tanks, manufacturing mass-transit cars instead of planes—then it would be possible (the possible good) to obtain a measure of disarmament.

Church leadership did find it possible to work successfully for the elimination of the draft—but this was true only because they did not push for elimination of all recruitment but instead were willing to accept the feasibility of a higher paid volunteer army (the possible good if you're going to have an army at all).

The Redemptive Initiative

Another method for resolving Christian decision-making is to seek out "the redemptive initiative." This seems to me a particularly manageable system for the layperson.

The system consists of a threefold process: (1) examine the problem; (2) analyze the question from the perspective of goals, intentions, means, and consequences; and (3) on the basis of this analysis, determine the redemptive initiative—that is, those initiatives which hold the most promise for benevolent change. The Christian basis for this might well be found in the purpose for which God sent Christ into the world. John 3:17 clearly points this out: "For God sent the Son into the world, not to condemn the world, but that the world might be saved through him." The Christian initiative has a "world-saving" objective. Christ's ministry reflects this in his encounters with Zacchaeus, with the woman at the well, with the rich young ruler. Successful or not, it is apparent that Jesus took those initiatives with persons which he felt might produce benevolent change. So, also, on the social scene we should seek out the redemptive initiative. Making sure one understands what the problem really is, subjecting it to careful analysis in the light of Christian principles, then asking oneself: What initiatives can be taken which will make a difference, which hold the promise of changing things for the better?

Perhaps the second step is the most agonizing in the process—the analysis from the Christian perspective. Are the long-range goals worthy? Are the intentions and motivations of participants honorable? Are the means appropriate? What are the likely consequences, and how are things likely to turn out considering various options?

Each portion of this analysis—goals, etc.—should be considered in the light of certain Christian principles, such as: (1) compassionate, imaginative understanding; (2) a healthy respect for realism; (3) obedience to Christ through justice and love; and (4) grace—the undeserved love of God.

In the limited space of this chapter, it is not possible to look at one social problem in comprehensive detail to see how the redemptive initiative might be applied. Nevertheless, let me at least hint at its application by applying the system to the energy crisis.

The Arab nations hold an overwhelming interest in world oil reserves and they have increased the price and, at least to some extent, limited the availability of oil. This was done partially to apply pressure toward a favorable solution in the Middle East. The Arab nations also undoubtedly saw the opportunity for greater revenue: they were keeping more of their oil in the ground at appreciating value.

What should the United States do about it? Needless to say, it is frightening to see such a strategic world commodity as oil used as a weapon. Furthermore, there is a deleterious effect on the Western world's economy, so dependent on oil and yet reluctant to pay excess prices which will hurt their foreign exchange.

When considering the U.S. goal, should it be to bring economic pressure, or military force, upon the Arab states to get them to roll back their prices? Or would it be more realistic to consider that over the long haul we should be developing alternate sources of energy? Should our intentions be primarily to punish the Arabs or to see that our limited supply of energy is equitably distributed? Is it more just as far as the U.S. citizenry is concerned to place higher prices on gasoline to cut consumption or to ration the gas supply? What would happen to the economies of Western Europe and Japan if their balance-of-payments situation considerably worsened as a result of paying increasingly high prices for Arabian oil? Will they experience inflation and recession? What effect does it have on the United States economy?

How will the energy crisis affect the poor? Will higher costs for fuel and gasoline price them out of the market? Also, since oil is used in making fertilizer and costs are likely to rise, will it be impossible to provide this commodity abroad for the developing nations just coming into the Green Revolution? There are many factors which must be assessed before making a decision based on justice and compassion while at the same time facing the moment of truth.

Then, where may we be pointed in determining the *redemptive initiative* on this issue? Certainly, whether popular or not, gasoline rationing would seem to be the fairest system for assuring a reasonably equitable distribution of available fuel. Also, substantial research and development of new sources of energy, such as solar, moving ahead on a crash basis would seem to be in order to provide just needs for all citizens. Meanwhile, in terms of stewardship, it would do all citizens some good to contemplate how energy might best be conserved and how the energy use trendline may be turned down. Also, consideration should be given to inaugurating efficient mass-transit systems to save fuel over the long run and at the same time to reduce air pollution.

As to our relations with Arab nations, perhaps some continuing discussions with Western nations would be appropriate, to convince them that destruction of the world's economy and monetary system would not be in their interests. Perhaps, in the name of promoting order in the international system, it would be helpful to encourage the United Nations to work out an agreement that *no* commodity should be used as a weapon against any other country in peacetime. At the same time, nations will need to find ways, through trade and other means, to become *interdependent,* not independent of one another. Only when such is true will the basis for a stable world peace exist.

§

As the prophetic community decides what is right for them to do on the social scene, they may wish to give consideration to one or more of the above social criteria in ethical decision-making. Or, occasionally, to step back and look at what they are doing from various perspectives of social ethics.

4.

FULFILLING THE PROPHETIC FUNCTION

Commitment to Advance Issues

The church can best fulfill its prophetic function by making a *conscious commitment to the advance issues*. Long before there was any War on Poverty, the prophet Amos made a commitment to seeking justice for the poor. The book of Jonah beautifully depicts the need for universal love in an age of self-centered nationalism. The wayward and hated Ninevites were the object of God's love despite the typical attitude represented by the provincial prophet Jonah. In II Isaiah, the advance issue was radical monotheism; that is, at their best the Hebrew people had always believed in one God, but now, during the Babylonian exile, they claimed that the God of other nations, even enemy nations, was Yahweh as well. Israel might not be the most powerful people, but her God was the most powerful—in fact he was the only God that existed! "I am God, and there is no other; I am God and there is none like me." (Isa. 46:7) In time, this radical monotheism changed the whole social outlook of Judaism.

What are some of the *advance issues* we see emerging today on the social scene? Some might be these:

—Whether or not the American Indians are to be given their rights.

- —Whether or not civil liberties, in the years just ahead, lie in jeopardy (the question of the right to privacy—the most reliable earmark of a civilized society—is being tested).
- —The question of *tax credits* and whether some devious device will be found that will permit private and parochial schools to be funded in large measure by public monies—a device that will skirt the "excessive entanglement" prohibited by the Supreme Court.
- —The issue of tax reform—whether some of the 54 items granting tax preferences shall be altered—such as tax-free bonds, accelerating depreciation, real estate and gift taxes, and capital gains, for example.
- —What kind of a system of national health care will be instituted in the United States over the next few years? Will it be comprehensive with a focus on preventive medicine? Can the U.S. continue to rank 14th in the rate of infant mortality among the industrial nations of the world? Or 18th in life expectancy of males?
- —Will an underground nuclear test-ban treaty be pursued? Or will new atomic weapons continue to be tested in the recesses of the earth, accelerating the arms race? Is there sufficient scientific advance in seismic equipment and enough confidence in the world community to take the leap of faith?
- —Despite the current energy crisis, will the U.S. support an international seabed authority under the U.N. and permit the use of the rich ocean resources (including oil) for international development purposes and U.N. peacekeeping costs, or will we decide to exploit the seabed's wealth unilaterally?

So, first, *commitment to advance issues.*

Form Task Forces

Second, a prophetic community, I think, would—as a practical matter—organize *a series of ad hoc task forces* relating to benevolent social change. Some might be in continuing fields—housing, education, welfare, drug rehabilitation, prison reform, etc. And some could relate to selected advance issues.

I would like to be quick to enter a disclaimer here regarding the prophets. They were loners, generally. Except for Jeremiah they were *not* organization men. But we simply must say that to implement their kind of worthy social objectives today requires more than a change of heart on the part of *the king.* In a democratic society one must relate broadly to leadership and to constituency.

Work with Secular Organizations

Third, the prophetic community would *work in cooperation with secular organizations on an issue* (but be ready to go it alone, if necessary).

Again, we must admit that the comparison of operating prophetically today with operating prophetically in ancient Hebrew times breaks down. For the prophets of the eighth and sixth centuries B.C. lived under a singularistic and more homogeneous structure. Their structures were basically religious—but they *did* relate to them.

This means then that the prophetic community, if it expects to be effective, will make some kind of a field force analysis and assess the strength of its adversaries on an issue; it will also determine its allies and then proceed to work with them.

Almost everything that is done by church representatives in Washington today is done through a coalition. Religious representatives themselves work closely together. Washington representatives of Catholic, Protestant, and Jewish organizations meet every two weeks for a whole morning and review the legislative picture. They also work together in implementing a legislative network called IMPACT and in reaching out into the key congressional districts.

Churches, at the national level, are today working with secular organizations in coalitions on housing, child care, handgun control, civil rights, the energy crisis, national priorities and foreign and military policy, comprehensive test-ban, use of the oceans, and U.N. issues—just to name a few. The walls keep changing but the people and organizations meeting in coalitions are often the same.

The Civil Rights Bill of 1964 brought the churches together in working with secular organizations in what turned out to be a successful operation. I know, for example, that on the key issue of stopping the filibuster in the senate, the Methodists attempted to relate to 22 senators, mostly Republican and mostly from the Midwest. When the final vote was taken, we found seventeen had voted right—for cutting off debate. But it wasn't simply because Methodists were encouraging favorable action; the constituents of many national organizations were relating to the same senators.

In 1966 I helped put together the first national gun-control organization in the country. The coalition involved came together in strength following the two assassinations in 1968 and achieved the limited objective of banning interstate mail-order sales of guns to individuals. Following that time, when the coalition weakened, the National Rifle Association won most battles.

One of the most interesting coalitions of recent vintage has been the Committee for Congressional Reform, organized in July of 1972. For many years we had seen creative, compassionate, benevolent legislation go down the drain and never really come before the congress because some powerful committee chairperson, acting arbitrarily and according to personal whim, sounded the death knell on a good bill. We were also disturbed that some 40% of the committee meetings were being held in secret. As Justice Brandeis once said: "Sunlight is said to be the best of disinfectants."[6] So the twin objectives were to change the systems of seniority and secrecy in the congress.

About fifty national organizations were brought into the coalition. In addition to some fifteen religious groups, the Congressional Reform organization included the League of Women Voters, Common Cause, Ralph Nader's Congressional Project, United Auto Workers, National Committee for Effective Congress, and a number of other public-interest organizations. Such a broad-based coalition had never been brought together before on an issue other than civil rights.

Private money was secured, staff hired, and a major victory achieved. This occurred when the Democratic Caucus of the House determined to vote on each chairperson separately and by secret ballot. This was done. So, what we now have in the house is a situation where chairpersons feel they are accountable to the whole party caucus for their actions and can no longer simply go their own merry way. They are subject to replacement regardless of their seniority. In addition, 95% of congressional committee meetings are open to the public.

This experience supports the validity and fundamental sensibility of the church working together with all secular allies who are congenial with an *ad hoc* objective.

Finally, I'm suggesting that a prophetic community truly performing its function will provide a *support mechanism* capable of maintaining morale.

For, at times, the struggle will be very lonely, full of discouragement, battered with criticism, and distressed by disappointment.

One will feel like Jeremiah:

> I did not sit in the company of merrymakers,
>   nor did I rejoice;
> I sat alone, because thy hand was upon me,
>   for thou hadst filled me with indignation.
> Why is my pain unceasing,
>   my wound incurable,
>   refusing to be healed?
> Wilt thou be to me like a deceitful brook,
>   like waters that fail?
>
> [Jer. 15:17-18]

Jeremiah was the only prophet who had disciples; they were helpful. When Jeremiah arranged to have his oracles read at the Temple courts, King Jehoiakim confiscated the scrolls and burned them. Jeremiah then simply dictated the oracles all over again to his disciple Baruch, and added a few extra words for good measure! His disciples were co-workers and helpfully supportive.

Thus, to avoid loneliness, task forces may have to come together occasionally to buttress one another. They can't all be failing at the same time.

5.

THE PROPHETIC COMMUNITY AND SOCIAL AND ECONOMIC AFFAIRS

Some of the prophets wandered from their home base. Amos, originally from Tekoa in the south, migrated to Israel and its larger cities in the north. There he fulfilled his prophetic function. Jeremiah may well have drifted (or been taken captive) into Babylon with the other exiles. Jesus, born in Bethlehem, according to tradition grew up in Nazareth and preached in Galilee, Samaria, and Judea.

But many of the prophets of the Old Testament stayed put. First Isaiah spent his entire ministry in and around Jerusalem. Second Isaiah remained with the exiles in the land of Babylon. When we come to the prophet of Nazareth, it is interesting to note that he made a desperate effort to relate his mission to his hometown (Luke 4:16-30). However, the record shows he was unsuccessful in inspiring his own hometown people to care about the poor, the blind, the oppressed, and those whose human rights had been violated and needed to be "set at liberty." In fact, they almost threw him off a nearby cliff. But he passed "through the midst of them."

In any case, if we are to fulfill the prophetic role, we too must seek to relate directly to the community at hand, expect to succeed, and take the risk of rejection. A neat catchy overstatement of fact, popular a few years ago, went: "All action is local." Yet that slogan was in a large measure true. Surely if persons do not relate to the community about them, where will they relate? There is no better place to start than in the local church, town or city. Everywhere there is enough useful, necessary benevolent work to go around.

The church has been at its best when it represented, not only a spiritual, pastoral, and evangelistic community, but also when it performed the role of *prophetic* community. One of the best examples of this was the Methodism of eighteenth- and nineteenth-century England—which surely could be described as an evangelistic movement. But the converted were gathered together in "Class Meetings." They worshiped and studied together in small groups of twelve or so. A collection was taken of one pence apiece for missionary work. The leader of the meeting would go around the circle and ask each one for a report of his or her accountability. "Sister Mary, how are you coming with teaching the street children how to read?" "Brother Andrew, can you use our help in your ministry to those in Fleet Street Prison?" "William, what can we do to assist you in your anti-slavery efforts?" "Sister Martha, would you be so kind as to report on your work at the medical dispensary?" And so it went. Each person was expected to be involved in some project of social significance—social service or social reform. When a person was "won for Christ," that person also became committed to a ministry in the name of Christ. The early Methodists were bright enough to know that if you only won persons to Christ who then went out to win others to Christ and so on, you might simply end up with a crowd in a large place. John Wesley Bready in his classic work *England: Before and After Wesley, The Evangelical Revival and Social Reform* (London: Hodder and Stoughton, 1938) gives early Methodism the credit for changing the face of England. They did it through the social outreach of the class meetings—the prophetic community in action. The drunken Parliament became sober. Public hangings were eliminated. The prisons were reformed. The public education movement was founded. By 1832 slavery throughout the British Empire was abolished.

Make-up of Prophetic Community

In any event, small groups meeting within the church today as the ongoing prophetic community could indeed make a tremendous impact upon our contemporary society. Even a little band of Christians operating within the church to promote social concern, social service, and social change may perform an exceedingly useful function. They don't have to be like-minded people, but they must be tolerant. They don't have to be convinced that everything each member of the group does or what the group itself undertakes is always correct. But they must be able to tolerate what others do to serve in the name of Christ if their own proposed projects are also to be considered. All those who operate within the prophetic community out of Christian motivation must be able to affirm life-supportive values. They don't have to all be liberals. Life-supportive values can also be affirmed by conservatives if, by that, they mean, for example, conserving life-supportive values of the past—such as keeping the water clean, the soil rich, and the air pure. Saving the best of our heritage could be the most prophetic thing that some groups could do. Stopping a strip-mining project which would seriously endanger the existence of a river or render land nonproductive could well be supported by a genuine and thoughtful conservative. Some radicals could make a useful contribution to the prophetic community. However, those radicals who believe that nothing useful can come in the way of social change without violent upheaval could be a problem. Extremists of the John Bircher stripe could also be a handicap if their only interest lies in engaging in anti-communist activities. "Status quo-ers" and obstructionists seldom make a contribution to those in the church who seek to adopt the prophetic role. There are always some persons who are unwilling to change anything in a community, especially if it costs money. They may be major property owners whose vision does not carry them beyond the next hike in taxes. Others are willing for their city or county taxes to rise if they are sure they are getting something worthwhile for it.

The Caring Community

The prophetic community within any church should be a *community of concern,* a caring community, a group of Christians who hold a deep concern over what happens to others in the church, the neighborhood, and the community. Sadly, citizens of the People's Republic of China have developed this community of mutual concern while Christians, too often, just talk about its virtues.

Senator Charles Percy of Illinois shares an illuminating incident which reflects upon the true nature of a community of concern. On a trip to mainland China, while visiting in a certain Chinese city, he noticed a thief stealing a child's bicycle. Immediately everyone on the street ran after the thief, caught him, and returned the bicycle to the child. The thief was not arrested and thrown into prison but was remonstrated with by the Chinese to make him aware of his lack of responsibility as a citizen of that community. The senator was amazed and said that this was not likely to happen in an American community. The people would be too busy—looking out for number one—or they would be afraid to act against crime or they would simply feel that it was the job of the police.

How we build a society in which we care enough about one another, starting within the church, is a matter of deep concern and far-reaching implication. Surely, the early church tended "the needs of the saints" (Rom.

12:13), but they also engaged in acts of healing and mercy and took care of the widows and fatherless. "They sold their possessions and goods, and distributed them to all, as any had need." (Acts 2:45) It should come as no surprise that "in Antioch the disciples were for the first time called Christians." (Acts 11:26) For it was in that city that, in the face of widespread famine, "the disciples determined, every one according to his ability, to send relief to the brethren who lived in Judea." (Acts 11:29) The prophetic community was at work.

Upon the 50th anniversary of the Menninger Foundation, a convocation was held in New York City entitled "Toward a Caring Society." Karl Menninger, the famous psychiatrist, said on that occasion that the key to helping healthy people achieve greater personal growth and fulfillment was to help people learn to care more for one another, personally and through institutions. Perhaps that is what we need to do through the institution of the church—create the "caring community." Are persons on hard drugs more likely to be able to overcome their dependence if they find help in a supportive community? Will mental patients be better able to come out of their schizophrenic state of withdrawal if a caring community is able to make it more comfortable for them to return to a life of facing reality? Would a prisoner given parole or a juvenile delinquent on probation be more likely to make it in straight society if connected with and surrounded by the love of a community of concern? Can you encourage the work of Alcoholics Anonymous by giving them space in your church, and by giving otherwise hopeless alcoholics the support of a caring community and religious faith and hope?

The redemptive potential of the prophetic community as a community of loving concern cannot be overestimated. It exists. It could have deep significance in relation to many of the most persistent and resistent problems which we face in American society.

Ideally the *whole* church should be the "prophetic community." But even if in reality it is represented by a tiny minority within the fellowship, like leaven in the lump, it will be of value. And if the whole church sees that you are doing some recognizable good, they will tolerate you; they might even applaud.

Working Alone Is Not Enough

We are constantly reminded that many in the church have adopted an individualistic approach to Christianity. They say: "Get a person's heart right and everything in society will turn out right." *That is pure bunk.*

Jesus has often been called the Prophet of Nazareth. He ranked in the prophetic tradition in that he sought benevolent change in society—the hungry poor were to be fed, the multitudes of sick were to be cured, the nation of Israel was to be spiritually liberated from their Roman oppressors. He called for a new moral rule in society—the coming of the kingdom of God. Compassion, health, freedom, a new structure—all were to be part of his social ministry and he was to be its instrument and the time was now.

True, the prophets of the Old Testament and Jesus acted as individuals. But one of the first things that Jesus did was to surround himself with disciples. And, after his death, these loyal followers were responsible for carrying forward a social ministry. That obligation continues to the current era.

The prophetic function, to be carried forward today, must be assumed by the corporate community, that is, by a group, and more specifically, by the church.

Private morality is important, and yet there are social forces at work today which cannot be effectively combatted by merely working alone. Groups of people must work together. And if ethics are going to be related to public-policy questions, what better instrument exists in our society than the church for such a purpose?

Take television, for example. Many parents feel helpless in the face of an overwhelming amount of violence on the screen today. The most popular adventure programs on TV are full of assault and murder. Now you can turn the set to the wall, or you can write an irate letter to the station or to a newspaper editor, but beyond that, what can you do as an individual? But the airwaves are public property: by FCC charter, the airwaves belong not to stations or to networks, but to the public, to *us*. This means that we can determine what goes on them—but only if we act together, as groups.

Or consider the question of crime. In a society where violent crime nationally remains at a high level, none of us can be sure that we will not be the victims of crime or that our children, adventurous and experimental as they often are, will not be victims of drugs.

One person working alone could relate somewhat haphazardly to crime. But a group of church persons who care could develop a system to help early delinquents to be shepherded away from a life of antisocial behavior and to bring those on probation and parole into a caring community of people who might help them to secure jobs, get counseling, and to meet other felt needs. Christian people working together can attack the conditions that breed crime. During the summer, in some of our cities it is estimated that young blacks and representatives of other minorities face an unemployment rate as high as 50%. Sociologists have often pointed out that the crime curve systematically follows the unemployment curve in its upward trend. What do we do to reduce unemployment which fosters crime?

Or consider the problem of world hunger. One person can do little to help prevent the starvation of millions of undernourished people around the world. But concerned Christians, acting together, can help substantially.

The churches of Ogle County in Illinois worked out a project to combat hunger through CROP (the Community Hunger Appeal of Church World Service). They used part of their weekends in November to glean the fields of the county—after the combines went through—picking up corn that had been left and donating it to CROP. This is a great program in which youth can be involved and achieve a sense of accomplishment. It could be duplicated in hundreds of counties throughout the United States.

What I have been saying here is that individuals working alone may be powerless to create benevolent social change. Evil forces at work in today's world are so powerful that they cannot be met successfully by individuals acting alone. But groups of concerned Christians informing themselves, full of resolve and imagination, may be able to successfully attack a problem and make our communities and our world a much better place to live in.

Too often in recent history personal concerns about religion have been separated out from social concerns. Up until the Civil War in our country evangelism and social concern were united within the church. According to Dr. Martin Marty, well-known church historian, it was only in the period after the Civil War that some churches began to stress one thing and others another. Consider the leading Abolitionists before the Civil War; they were also great evangelists.

Do you realize that it was the churches directly after the Civil War that were responsible for eliminating dueling from our society? Up until that time it was a common social custom. We know about honorable men, such as Alexander Hamilton and Abraham Lincoln, being involved in this barbarous practice. In the atmosphere of a general revulsion against violence after the bloody Civil War, the churches were successful in getting dueling outlawed. Nobody thinks about it today. If someone came up to us today and said, "I hereby challenge you to a duel," the normal response would be to laugh in their face. Not so before the Civil War. The churches changed all that by their corporate social action.

Taking a Poll in the Church

There are some lovely people in the church today who firmly believe that the church should take no action on an issue without first taking a poll of its members. It is not a bad idea to occasionally take surveys of opinions of people in the church—just to know where they stand. But this should not serve as a bar to action. If the church has to wait for the last foot-dragging member to give approval to a social-service or social-action project, it is in serious trouble. Being a prophetic community means being out in front, demonstrating leadership and not just engaging in activities that are widely popular and "safe."

If Amos had had to wait until he achieved a consensus before proclaiming his prophetic utterances at Bethel, he no doubt would have remained a silent partner with God. Or if Jesus had taken a poll in his hometown on whether or not he should engage in his social ministry to Galilee, Samaria, and Judea, judging by the reception of his first sermon by the townspeople, he never would have been heard of beyond Nazareth.

Jesus as a Model

Some friends in the church object to social-concern activity because, they say, "Jesus never did it." If that is the criterion, we are in serious trouble. For on the basis of this determination:

- —we should not be concerned about juvenile delinquents—because Jesus never met one;
- —we should certainly not care about the some 50,000 alcohol-related traffic fatalities each year—since Jesus rode only on a donkey;
- —we should never be concerned about the problem of war—since Jesus didn't speak of it, living as he did in a period of enforced peace—the "Pax Romana."

Taking Jesus' *acts* as our *only* mandate for action would be a serious mistake, resulting in a spiritually stifling experience. What we are really after is the spirit of Christ—his compassion, mercy, sense of justice—seeking then to relate this to the whole of life, personal and social.

It would be unusual in the church if certain persons did not think a one-to-one social ministry quite satisfactory and yet object to any action by an official church body that confronted the social system. However, we have at least one account (surprisingly found in all four Gospels) in which Jesus did just that. In cleansing the Temple of the moneychangers, Jesus attacked the most callous profit-making racket existing in Jerusalem at that time. The Sadducees and priests were making huge profits from the exorbitant prices on animals sold for Temple sacrifice and from selling certain coins especially minted for the Temple head tax.

It was this opposition to corruption that brought Jesus into direct conflict with the religious hierarchy and sealed his death. It's all right to give nature talks on lilies of the field, entertain people with parables, heal a few of the miserable sick, and correct a few outcast sinners. But if you want to stay out of trouble, for goodness sake don't attack a profitable and corrupt social system. Yet Jesus did.

Community Problems

Where does the prophetic community tie in? Certainly, it doesn't just get motivated, lower its head, and charge into things like a bull in a china shop. The group will review the areas where it could make some kind of social impact. Is there a pollution problem in the community? Some terrible odors? Chemical dumping in the river? Sulphur spewing into the sky? Does the city have a drug-abuse problem of serious proportions? Do working mothers need more quality child-care facilities? Is school busing an issue? Is there any racial tension? In your county is agribusiness taking over the family farms? Are the elderly adequately cared for? Is unemployment a difficult problem in your area? Does sufficient lower-income housing exist, and is mortgage money available to minorities and to low- and middle-income families? Is "red-lining" by the local bank a prevailing practice? Are the recreation needs of the community adequate? Is there a program to rehabilitate juvenile delinquents? Is there any labor-management strife? Are there persons in the community facing hunger or malnutrition?

The social-concerns group will want to review questions like this. If there are at least a dozen in the basic "prophetic community," it might well pay for each person in the group to survey ten persons in the town or county and ask questions like the above—but selected by the group itself. Then, at a subsequent meeting, if all were to report back giving comments from respondents, it would help the organization to decide where to start.

Getting Organized

Surely, it would be wise to begin by relating to a commonly recognized problem and with a problem that is reasonably manageable. Although it might be best to start off with a project that could carry broad support—like hunger or delinquency or pollution control—it is important to decide from the beginning that controversy will not be avoided. Some of the most fascinating and valuable projects will be those which do raise more than eyebrows from the opposition. Harmless as your intent may seem to be, dealing with the sulphur-belching smokestacks could bring you into direct conflict with the owner of the plant who may be a church member and also a large contributor. When you oppose poor housing in the community, you may find it owned by the husband of the organist. The "red-lining" operation at the bank could be under the direction of an officer who will decide whether or not the bank will grant a loan for the church addition. The possibilities are endless for being cowed into doing nothing.

For this reason it is important to be informed, to report periodically to the whole congregation, to involve as many as possible from the entire church in your project, and to proceed cautiously but with assured determination. Committee assignments may need to be made. Occasionally this may involve a bit of "log-rolling"—that is: "I'll support your project if you support mine." Presumably, both projects are fully acceptable to the prophetic community.

Money may have to be raised. Don't hesitate to ask for support from the regular budget, and make it possible also for persons to designate gifts to your project. Your program may be just as important to the life of the church as building some new chapel, landscaping the church, buying more hymnals, or purchasing summer robes for the choir. Many persons in the church want to give their funds to something meaningful that produces obvious positive and beneficial results. They should periodically be given that opportunity.

When it comes right down to it, what do you do? In the back of this book are listed more than 100 possible projects from various faiths all over the country which may serve as models for your particular prophetic community. Have your group run over these and write to several for further information. What these people are doing *has* worked; maybe it will work for you.

To give you a few examples of what is going on around the nation in the name of the Christian community, let me mention a few.

Handyperson Home Maintenance Service

I am impressed by the great variety of projects which are being implemented under the auspices of the Interfaith Community Services of St. Joseph, Missouri. They conduct many social services on an interfaith and interdenominational basis, including day-care centers, mobile meals, a senior citizens center, child advocacy, and housing programs. But one of the more unusual initiatives they have undertaken is the Handyperson Home Maintenance Service (see page 109). This is a program designed to benefit both the elderly homeowner or apartment dweller with maintenance or repair problems and the retired person who needs some additional income or who simply wants to help others.

The main idea is to make it possible for the elderly to remain in their homes by providing assistance with the upkeep of their property. So if a doorknob falls off and their hands are too arthritic to fix it, there's someone available with a screwdriver. There are simple things around an apartment or a house which can easily go wrong and if not repaired may mean that an elderly couple will have to move out of familiar surroundings and into a home for the aging. How many persons come to the place where they must say regretfully: "I just couldn't keep the place up anymore." The kind of assistance that Handyperson Home Maintenance is providing could be duplicated by churches in most communities. Simple, but valuable.

The Garden Patch

The Church of the Brethren of Root River, in Preston, Minnesota, has a project (see page 167) that could be duplicated in most town and rural areas. Their hunger-related project is called "The Garden Patch"; it is a weekly halfday marketplace for excess garden produce from local gardens in the community. Each week several families, from both the church and the larger community, bring in items to sell at the Garden Patch. The Patch is actually a booth located near a local supermarket where townspeople can purchase what they like at about half the current market price. Income from the project is used to support local and world hunger programs. The effort also gives local residents, often the elderly, an opportunity to buy fresh fruits and vegetables at prices they can afford. The local supermarket provides the booth and even buys the excess produce for the day. Some of the excess is often given to a local hospital/nursing home and a halfway home for retarded adults. Any small rural church could use the Garden Patch as a model for outreach on the world hunger emphasis now popular in churches.

Housing Opportunity Association

One attractive model project (see page 157) in the field of housing for lower-income families is the Housing Opportunity Association of Bethlehem, Pennsylvania. This program, initiated with five volunteer directors and $1,000 in 1968, grew by 1978 into a program that currently places 18 families in homes under agreement of sale with the occupants. HOA now has 12 directors and does not plan to have more than 25 families in its housing at any one time so as to keep the work load within bounds and retain the voluntary character of the organization.

The project is housed in the facilities of the First Presbyterian Church of Bethlehem, which also makes a financial contribution and provides secretarial services. The Housing Opportunity Association board accepts and evaluates applications from families encountering difficulty in finding housing. As its funds permit, it helps those families with the greatest need and also with the potential of becoming self-sufficient. Usually these families do not qualify for either public housing or private mortgages. They have been unable to obtain adequate rental housing within their means.

After determining a family's housing needs, HOA finds a home, obtains a mortgage from a local bank, makes renovations, then enters into an agreement with the family. If the family agrees to purchase the home with HOA's help, then the Housing Opportunity Association's investment is regarded as a loan which the family repays in a monthly payment that includes the bank mortgage and interest. Each applicant is expected to have saved $500 toward the down payment. HOA lends the remainder of the down payment money at 6%. When the loan is fully repaid, HOA transfers the title and remaining mortgage to the family which then assumes the responsibility of home ownership in the usual sense. The Housing Opportunity Association makes a special effort to help those families who may have been discriminated against because of race or family size.

The directors are members of several churches, Protestant and Catholic. Three churches contribute to the Housing Opportunity Association's housing fund, and so do 85 private donors of various faiths.

I think it is possible that churches in most towns and cities could reproduce a project like that of the Housing Opportunity Association. Do you have persons who are dedicated volunteers? Can you scrape $1,000 together? Then you would be where HOA was in 1968 when they launched their project.

Koinonia Medical Center

An interesting program first initiated in churches and conducted under the leadership of a Christian layman is the Koinonia Medical Center (see page 146). The kernel of the idea came when Dr. Dale L. Williams, a United Methodist physician and former missionary, started holding several "well-baby clinics" in various churches of Muskegon, Michigan. As time went on, certain indigent adults from the community came and said: "We need a doctor too."

So Dr. Williams organized the Koinonia Medical Center in Muskegon Heights. He and his associates secured a building reasonably accessible to their expected clientele—largely the poor who were unable to get appointments with private physicians. Before Koinonia, the people of this area were limited to medical care at hospital emergency rooms during emergencies. This did not include prenatal care, ongoing child care, or care for the continuing needs of adults and the elderly. Koinonia has been based on the passage in Matthew 25:40 where Jesus said: "Inasmuch as ye have done it unto one of the least of these my brethren, ye have done it unto me." (KJV)

Starting out with a small staff, Koinonia now has six doctors (part-time), two physician assistants, and two nurses. The Center's motto is: "No one will be turned away for lack of funds." Most have Medicaid and Medicare or they pay a small fee in accordance with their income. Initiated in 1973, the Koinonia Medical Center now serves between 120 and 150 persons a day and has outgrown its quarters. Among the services offered are: general medical care, complete examinations, laboratory services, obstetrical care, office surgery, prenatal care, parents classes, allergy treatment, pediatric consulting, planned-parenthood clinics, and home calls to homebound convalescents. Family counseling is conducted under the leadership of Reverend Benjamin Ypma. The physician assistants, who are trained paramedics, conduct all the physical checkups and any follow-ups. Only the doctors, however, are permitted to diagnose illnesses.

Do the poorer people of your community have a medical need? Is there at least one physician committed to serving such needs at a sacrifice? Perhaps a Koinonia Center is the order of the day.

Good Samaritan Association

A particularly winsome program is one called the "Good Samaritan Association" (see page 172) which originated in the spring of 1974 in the Sacred Heart Roman Catholic Church of San Diego, California. It is composed entirely of volunteers, modern-day Samaritans who devote time through their outreach programs to help persons in need. They seek to give freely of their time and talents, spiritual and temporal, to minister to the needs of the poor and lonely.

Through their Financial Assistance program, the Good Samaritans provide emergency aid for such items as rental and cleaning deposits due to relocation, installation charges of utility bills, medicines, clothing, and bus and plane fares. Their Emergency Food program responds to the calls of hungry single adults, families, and the elderly with prepackaged, nonperishable food. Through Home Visitation, the Samaritans stay with persons returned home from the hospital, shop for food for the elderly, visit the lonely, and provide social activities for the development of companionship.

With an annual income of only about $4,000, these volunteers accomplish a great deal, especially as they relate to the elderly—who are generally in their 80s and trying to live independently in various neighborhood communities. For example, in one week's time the group supported elderly persons in the following ways:

—paid for pest-control service.

—set up a fund for a terminally ill patient.

—cleaned an apartment for a disabled patient.

—visited and prepared lunch for a disabled woman on weekdays.

—paid a delinquent phone bill to avoid termination of service.

—paid for TV repairs, TV being the only source of entertainment.

—purchased and installed a safety brace in the home of a homebound arthritic client.

—made routine home visitation by the outreach team.

—gave support to several social-service agencies in San Diego.

—made two emergency food deliveries.

Reflects Rose Ebner, director of Good Samaritans: "Within this busy week of diversified calls, we found time to laugh and pray together, wipe a tear away and urge a smile, all the while aware of the continuing presence of Jesus Christ."

Certainly most small prophetic communities where there are a few volunteers available would find it possible to use the Good Samaritan Association as a model. The poor, lonely, and elderly await Samaritan help everywhere.

Full Employment Project

The Full Employment Project (see page 112) of the Des Moines Area Urban Mission Council is surely an unusual one. This United Methodist-sponsored program experimented with the concept that the unemployed would be able to help one another get jobs. They hired an Organizer/Job Developer, Bob Jackson, a talented black who had been unemployed for the previous year. Mr. Jackson organized over 100 unemployed persons into a "Jobless United" group. The purpose of the group was to aid one another in seeking employment, to develop job opportunities with the employment sector, to aid in job-training opportunities, and to help one another in eliminating common barriers to finding suitable employment.

The membership of "Jobless United" varied greatly in ethnic background, education, and employment experience. Over a six-month period—November 1977 to May 1978—thirty-six persons were placed for employment. These included jobs in such work as construction, factories, insurance companies, discount stories, school maintenance, hospitals, restaurants, etc.

In addition, a support group was formed of concerned citizens from the religious community, employment organizations, and other interested citizens. This organization, known as the Full Employment Coalition, formulated guidelines for the organizer, hunted jobs, and ferreted out funding for the project. Funding sources included the United Presbyterian Church, the Catholic Church, the United Methodist Church, the United Auto Workers, and the National Council of Churches.

This exemplary initiative could be duplicated in other city areas. What seems to be required is funding for a competent organizer and a prophetic community group ready to volunteer some time to the unemployment issue.

Ministry of Criminal Justice

One of the more exciting and successful programs in the criminal justice field is the Ministry of Criminal Justice sponsored by United Methodists in Illinois. Funding is provided by the church, the Illinois Department of Corrections, and private gifts. Staff consists of seven full-time members and three part-time members with more than 300 volunteers throughout the state of Illinois. The philosophy of the criminal justice program rests on the concept that no corrections or criminal justice system can fulfill its expectations without the total involvement of the community.

Lying at the heart of the Ministry's program is an operation called "Communities Upholding Persons" (C.U.P.). The focus of this program is upon the local county and its criminal justice system. C.U.P. recruits local persons who become involved with offenders and their families at the point of their need. They also educate the community about the problems of the criminal justice system and the role they could play in their neighbors' lives. The goal of a C.U.P. volunteer is to attempt to assist offenders to readjust and reintegrate into their respective communities upon release. The program contends: "If we express concern for a person while he/she is locked in, then maybe . . . they will care when they get out." As one resident of the Vienna Correctional Center in southern Illinois put it: "Would you rather meet me now, or maybe in a dark alley someday in the future?"

C.U.P. believes that certain offenders can derive benefit from one-to-one relationships with carefully selected and trained citizen volunteers. Offenders are not all alike. Thus volunteers are carefully assigned so they are most likely to succeed in relating effectively with a given offender. Some offenders are not considered potential candidates for a helpful one-to-one relationship. For instance, it was discovered early that volunteers were not effective in working with severely disturbed residents.

C.U.P. volunteers perform a variety of functions as they relate to county-jail residents. They visit residents and their families, engage in public relations, maintain a library and a canteen in the county jail, assist with employment and educational development, provide for housing assistance, help put out a monthly newsletter, and speak at churches, colleges, and service organizations. The Reverend William Johnson, Executive Director for Ministry of Criminal Justice, explains: "The overall responsibility of all volunteers is that they do for the resident/ex-offender what he cannot do; they do not help the resident/ex-offender in what he is capable of doing."

While a resident is incarcerated, C.U.P. seeks to aid and support the inmate's family, too. Whether it is being a shoulder to cry on, taking a sick child to the doctor, babysitting for a working mother, or providing transportation to the prison to see their loved one, C.U.P. is ready to become involved.

During a recent year, 225 C.U.P. volunteers served in relationships with about 1,000 high-risk offenders. Volunteers have ranged in age from 18 to 74 with the average being about 32. About 70% were women and about 80% of the volunteers were married. The average educational level was 15 years. Almost all hold a religious affiliation. Various walks of life are represented: blue-collar workers, professors, housewives, plumbers, attorneys, college students, and retirees. About 85% of the volunteers assigned to a one-to-one relationship agree to be reassigned. The average age of the residents/ex-offenders C.U.P. deals with is about 28, and about 98% of them are male. No special problems have arisen due to the ratio of male residents to female volunteers.

Is the program effective? Hear what Sheriff L. L. Kimmel of Whiteside County attests: "I have been in law enforcement for nearly eighteen years and associated with corrections and jails for twelve of those years. C.U.P. is without a doubt the most viable program for jails that I have ever had the pleasure to be associated with."

One thing is certain: C.U.P. and the Ministry of Criminal Justice programs are the prophetic community at work. They are Christians working together to love persons in trouble back to life. Christian churches in many other states could use this program as an action model. (For more information and address, see page 134.)

St. Mary's Food Bank

Surely one of the most ambitious church-sponsored projects in the nation must be the St. Mary's Food Bank Salvage Program of Phoenix, Arizona. So successful has this program been that in the spring of 1978 they hosted the first National Food Bank Conference. While it is true that this kind of program works best in cities of a considerable size, many county areas would find it possible to duplicate the broad outlines of the project.

The St. Mary's Food Bank Salvage Clearinghouse is based on the premise that what the Department of Agriculture says about food losses in America is true—that $31 billion worth of food is wasted yearly. This amounts to 137 million tons of otherwise usable supplies.

Through the initiative of John Van Hengel, a volunteer working for a local social agency, the St. Mary's Food Bank was established in 1967. Mr. Van Hengel, who went on to become the volunteer director, realized at that time that there were many people in the area who were hungry and yet, at times, charity agencies had a surplus of food; at other times they had none. What was needed was a food bank where, in times of surplus, food could be stored.

Through the help of a friend, Father Ronald Colotty of St. Mary's Church, John Van Hengel was able to locate a headquarters for St. Mary's Food Bank—an old warehouse on South Central Street. To stock the Food Bank, John contacted bakeries and food plants to ask for day-old bread and surplus. He went to grocery chains to ask for damaged and non-salable food. He asked for promotion through the local media.

He found shelving, food cases, and walk-in freezers to store the food until it could be distributed. He recruited volunteers from the agencies that were to receive his services, and set up a system for the agencies and organizations to distribute food to the needy.

In its first year of operation the nondenominational Food Bank distributed 250,000 pounds of salvage food. By 1975, 1,800,000 pounds of food were being distributed at an annual cost of less than $15,000 total. No salaries were being paid. The main trick is to gather salvageable food, such as: outdated products, day-old bakery goods, dented canned goods, broken packaging, shrinkage ice cream, bruised meat products, seconds in produce, etc.

Through an exchange program called Second Harvest, food that is in surplus is exchanged with similar food banks in the southwestern and western states. Locally 237 charities, social workers, and churches participate in the program. 25,000 three-day food boxes have been distributed annually throughout Phoenix. No government funding or interference is involved. The Food Bank's motto is: "The poor we shall always have with us, but why the hungry?" (For address, see page 163.)

Energy Conservation Campaign

One possible project that would be current, relevant, and meaningful for participants would be local involvement in the Energy Conservation Campaign. This campaign is sponsored by the Interfaith Coalition on Energy (I.C.E.) of Washington, D.C. I am secretary of I.C.E. and therefore acquainted with its activities.

Hundreds of local congregations across the nation have been participating in the Energy Conservation Campaign. Participation fundamentally means that local churches undertake to get their members to covenant together regarding specific ways that energy may be saved. After this question is discussed in one way or another, persons in the church commit themselves with respect to twelve items listed on a Covenant Card. A portion of the card is mailed into I.C.E. for future presentation to the president in a ceremony and the congregant keeps a duplicate portion reminding the member of the commitment made.

I.C.E. leaders believe that if a large portion of the 100 million members of churches and synagogues would seriously seek to conserve, it would be possible to save at least 10% of the total energy consumption in the country. Some 35% of national usage consists of those items under the control of families: 21% is consumed by households and 14% by the automobile. Therefore, it is important for Christian families not to just blame the oil companies or the Arabs, but to say to themselves: "How can we help resolve the energy crisis as we try to exercise our stewardship responsibility in connection with scarce resources?"

As the Energy Conservation Campaign indicates, there are many little ways that, totaled up, would save huge quantities of energy. Some of these include car pooling, purchasing energy efficient appliances, turning off unnecessary lights, or turning down the temperature on the hot water heater.

Let us just look at one item—the last one above. What if all the families living in owner-occupied homes in the United States turned their hot water heaters down from 140 to 110 degrees Fahrenheit. This would cause little problem for the family other than having unsterilized dishes. Who needs them sterilized? So, with a twist of the wrist, moving the dial from "hot" to "warm" on the hot water unit, it would be possible to save the equivalent of 75 million barrels of oil per year in the U.S.A. That would amount to seven days a year of total oil imports.

Thus it is that, through modest and reasonable steps requiring little sacrifice, it would be possible to save meaningful amounts of fuel. Why shouldn't Christians take the lead? Christ focused on the stewardship theme as often as any other in his teaching through parables. ". . . To whom much is given, of him will much be required." (Luke 12:48)

Any size church could involve itself in this kind of mission. Also, a group of churches in a community could covenant together on a conservation program. For a packet of materials to help implement your Energy Conservation Campaign (including a Covenant Card), send 25 cents to the Interfaith Coalition on Energy, 236 Massachusetts Avenue, N.E., Washington, D.C. 20002.

From the wide range of possible projects listed at the back of this book, perhaps your prophetic community could select one as a possible model, adding your own adaptation and flavor to it. It doesn't have to be terribly ambitious; it can start out small, just an idea. If insufficient resources are a problem, don't hesitate to invite other churches in to share with volunteers and funding. Also, sometime in the future, it may be that the community itself will want to take over your project. This should be an occasion for pride and delight, not shame. For as the churches launched most of the hospitals and colleges in the country which have any history, so we can expect that projects initiated by churches in our own day will be secularized.

§

An important factor in the successful development of any community project is its periodic evaluation. After six months or a year, take a look at it. Check back in your minutes to see if the original purposes are being achieved. Is there any progress? How has the project changed from its original conception? Where are the "loose spots"? Does it have public support? What has been its image? Also, ask outsiders what their conception of the project is. Check it out with beneficiaries. Is anyone being helped? As Jesus said: "By their fruits you shall know them."

Don't get discouraged if progress is slow and the cause is yet just. But don't be afraid to admit that another route might be better for the sponsoring group. On the other hand, if you have some successes, don't be afraid to celebrate. One of the most expendable commodities is the sour prophetic community!

6.

THE PROPHETIC COMMUNITY AND POLITICAL AFFAIRS

To the right of the entrance of the Dirksen Senate Office Building on Capital Hill is a huge bronze plaque acknowledging the senators on the building committee. A few steps further to the left in a dark alcove is a tiny plate with the words "In God We Trust."

Too often religious values are hidden in the alcoves of congress. It is imperative to relate Christian ethics to the decisions made by our legislators who are subject to many selfish pressures.

Political action in today's world is the most powerful means by which social change takes place.

When one views
- —the social consequences of the Civil Rights Bill of 1964,
- —the increasing job potential for blacks and women as a result of giving enforcement powers to the Equal Employment Opportunity Commission in 1971,
- —the likelihood of a more sensitive and conscientious congress as a result of modification of the seniority system and the opening up of congressional committees to the public in 1974,

then one can only conclude that effective political decision-making will often result in far-reaching, positive, substantive changes in the social scene.

Losing One's Innocence by Getting Involved

But how does the prophetic community relate to this? Isn't there supposed to be a separation of church and state?

In Book I of Plato's *Republic,* Socrates offers a pithy truism when he says: "The penalty that good people pay for not being interested in politics is to be governed by persons worse than themselves."[7] Too many Christians, however, believe that if they become politically involved, it necessarily means dirtying their hands and corrupting their souls.

Yet when Jesus faced a corrupt system of moneychanging in the Temple, he did not say, "It's none of my business." Instead he went about his Father's business by ridding Jerusalem of a scandal that enjoyed the silent approval of the political and religious authorities. Jesus was not a *purist* fearful of staining his soul through involvement with the real world.

The church today must not remove itself from the real world of political decisions even if it risks making mistakes or damaging its image when it is wrong. For some church persons an issue must be all pure and undefiled by the world. Such issues may be hard to find.

Let's face it. Through political action, it is very seldom that you can fight slums without hurting slumlords (who could be good church members!). It is seldom that you will be able to provide for school integration through necessary busing without making some parents angry (white and black). You aren't going to clean up rivers without imposing regulations on building developers who constantly disturb the soil and allow it to wash down into the water.

Some kindhearted Christian people get involved in noble political-action ventures but soon find they are tramping on the toes of neighbors. Then they cry out: "But I was only trying to do some good!" What they didn't realize was that in "doing good" some persons may get hurt and consider such benevolence as troublemaking. Jesus must have known that if he did good by ridding the Temple of moneychanging, somebody would hate him for it. The moneychangers undoubtedly said: "What does he mean by putting us out of work! Who will feed our families?"

Issues that cost nothing and make nobody mad are hard to find. Let us remind ourselves again of Dr. Harvey Seifert's observation: "Working for the 'impossible perfect' instead of the 'possible good', simply means donating the victory to whomever is supporting the 'possible bad.' "[8]

Separation of Church and State

Others in the church object to the church's getting into political issues on strict doctrinaire grounds of separation of church and state. Such persons remind us that the First Amendment states: "Congress shall make no law respecting an establishment of religion." They believe that the wall of separation should remain high. They see the danger of the church becoming a political party.

Actually, however, the concept means that the state should not dominate the church (as it did at the height of Hitler's power in Germany), nor should the church dominate the state. As history revealed to us through Calvin's Geneva experiment, when you invest the church with national authority and police power, it becomes oppressive.

This is not to say that the state cannot have an influence upon the church. Nor should the church be prevented from attempting to exercise a benevolent influence upon the state. Indeed, the church is obligated to make the effort. Not to do so would be irresponsible. All kinds of influences bear upon the decision-making apparatus of the government. Many of these influences are exercised for provincial, purely selfish, purposes. For the church not to act out of the highest motivation in the interests of all of God's children would be disastrous. It would permit a moral vacuum into which the apostles of private aggrandizement would rush, to the appalling disadvantage of the public.

Many church members feel that they have no business relating to the state since high government officials have access to more up-to-date, accurate, and sometimes secret information, not available to the ordinary citizen. Yet Dr. Hans Morgenthau, eminent political science professor from the University of Chicago, dispels such a notion. The highly respected academic in years past has been one of the State Department's closest advisors and has had access to such privileged information. In response to those who say, "But I haven't got all the facts," the professor has asserted that it isn't "all the facts" that the president or the common citizen needs to make decisions. What are needed, says Morgenthau, are "the relevant facts." In our day of mass media and rapid news coverage, except for emergency situations, these are available to the ordinary person who seeks them.

How to Organize Locally

If one makes a decision to organize in the local church for political action, how would one go about it?

The first requirement would be to assemble a group of motivated people (the prophetic community) who would favor the Christian faith moving beyond worship and study to effective social action. It is important, of course, to be spiritually oriented and knowledgeable, but it is also important to be "doers of the word." Even if there are only a half dozen persons who are willing to meet regularly with the ultimate objective of acting themselves and encouraging political action by other church persons, this would be enough.

Such a group at the outset ought to be very clear about the difference between social education, social service, and social change. Let me illustrate with one example—child care. A worthy church program might be for a group to make a study of the problems of working mothers, of the neglected preschool child, and of the need for child-care facilities. This would be social education. A worthwhile church project might be to set up a preschool nursery for use by working mothers. This would represent social service. But another approach might be to organize action on behalf of federal legislation to provide funds and guidelines to establish critically needed child-care facilities nationwide. This would move into the area of social change. Or to be more specific, such social change would be sought through *political action* to change the system.

Though the political-action group may be small within a church, it should nevertheless be influential. For unless it is composed of persons who are respected in the church, its attempts to get other members to act will fall on deaf ears. Also, some balance might be sought on the committee—some youth, some women, some minorities, some Republicans as well as Democrats, some moderates (and conservatives in the true sense of the word) as well as liberals. In any event, they need to be people who are not afraid of social change so long as it is benevolent change. Sometimes such change costs money and may mean new taxes. Thus, if the political-action committee is dominated by persons who want only change that is economically painless, the prophetic community's work in this area will probably be thwarted.

Also, the committee should recognize that, in all of its major projects, it will need to carry the church membership with it. It cannot be thought of as "that little band of radical activists who are giving our church a bad name." The committee will be initiators, but in most projects not implementers acting alone. They will involve others from the membership.

What Issues to Deal With?

The group may wish to limit itself to only two or three policy issues for the first year or so. In the beginning it might be best to engage in working on issues that are not highly controversial and on ones where it is possible to have some success.

Whatever issue is selected, committee members will have to inform themselves with respect to the facts. If it is a local issue, this may require attending city or county council meetings and reporting to the group. Or it may necessitate interviewing key persons familiar with the issue and drawing some conclusions. Someone may have to engage in independent research and make a report.

Then comes the time for ethical analysis. How are Christian values related to this issue? How does one decide what is right and wrong about a controversial question? For a discussion of this, look back to chapter 3.

How to Relate Ethics to Power

Once a position has been agreed to by the prophetic community and an ethical analysis has been made, then appropriate action should be determined to bring about favorable results. This may mean testifying before the county or city council. One word of caution—do not testify on behalf of your church unless you have received approval from the governing body of the church. There is nothing wrong with making a witness on behalf of a modest group of concerned Christians within the church—as long as you make it clear you are simply representing yourselves.

On local issues, forums before the congregation may be useful. Getting an article or a series of articles in the town or county newspaper could help the cause. Make friends with the editor. If there is a local radio or TV station, seeing that a public question is fairly discussed ought to have a high priority.

Since in my daily work I relate to national legislation, a large part of this section will deal with how to relate effectively to the United States government on national issues. Nevertheless, the same principles apply to state issues. In some cases, there is even an important intertwining between national and state issues—as in the case of the Equal Rights Amendment, which passed the congress as a Constitutional Amendment and is now in the process of gradually being ratified by two-thirds of the state legislatures.

Suppose the prophetic community decides to try to become more effective at influencing legislative issues, what would it do? First, being informed about the issues is essential, whether they are national issues or local.

Reading a good daily paper helps; also, reading a news magazine regularly. For an ethical flavor, season your information with a periodical which tends to look at public issues from an ethical perspective. *Engage/Social Action* magazine, *A.D.*, and *The Christian Century* are good models for this.

As the next step, responsible Christian citizens may be ready for the one-two-three aspects of current bills before the congress. Some specific knowledge of how a bill moves through the legislative process may be helpful. For a guide to what ordinarily happens to a bill before the congress, ask your representative for a pamphlet entitled *How Our Laws Are Made.*

To know where a bill is specifically in the legislative hopper, consult the *Congressional Record* or the *Congressional Quarterly Weekly Report.* The *Record* (a daily) is inexpensive enough so that an individual or a church interested in obtaining it could subscribe. It costs just $45 a year. A daily digest, printed at the back of the *Congressional Record,* provides the reader with the substance of what is going on as well as page numbers for more detailed information. However, one thing should be made clear. Just because something is printed in the *Congressional Record* does not mean it is *true*. Every member of congress has the right to enter all kinds of material coming from constituents into the *Record*.

The *Congressional Quarterly* (actually a weekly) gives a detailed analysis of issues, bills, hearings, and of the legislative and electoral processes. Unfortunately, since a subscription costs several hundred dollars a year, most churches will have to seek it out at the public library.

Another essential means for the group to inform itself on the issues is to know the voting record of congresspersons and senators. There are two good sources for this data: *Voting Record,* published annually by IMPACT (110 Maryland Avenue, N.E., Washington, D.C. 20002) and *Voting Record and Review,* put out each year by the Friends Committee on National Legislation (245 Second Street, N.E., Washington, D.C. 20002). Both resources provide the votes of members of congress on about 15 key issues, together with an explanation of the issue.

Knowing how your congressperson voted on particular issues will help your committee in certain ways. You can compliment your representative on votes when you are in agreement. You can learn your representative's views in certain areas—such as civil rights, welfare issues, or peace questions. In this way you will know whether the congressperson you will be communicating with is liberal or conservative. Also, if the legislative voting record is absolutely contrary to your view of Christian principles, you may be forced to conclude that your representative (or senator) should be replaced.

Christians have to think ahead about what the issues are likely to be in the future. For example, one of the major issues during the next several years may be national health insurance.

By the early 1980s it is quite likely that all Americans will live under some form of national health care. Will that plan be comprehensive and include preventive features? How will services be delivered? What are the costs likely to be and how will these costs be met? Who will administer the health plan? The prophetic community ought to engage now in reasonable and ethical decision-making dealing with such questions.

After the concerned Christian community has identified the significant policy issues, studied the legislation, and obtained a reading on their legislators, what more can be done? Bishop G. Bromley Oxnam, former Methodist bishop of the Washington Area, used to say: "If church people are going to be effective on public issues, they must register Christian opinion with the persons making the decisions before the decisions are made."

Letter writing is one of the easiest and most effective ways to communicate views to members of congress, the decision-makers. Effective members of the prophetic community will find ways to encourage other church members to write letters to congress. A letter need not be long. It is well to keep it reasonably brief, to the point, and on one issue. Raise intelligent questions which cannot be answered with the usual form letter. Express moral concern where appropriate, and share information and research you have which bears on the particular question. And remember, timing is extremely important. Arrange for letters to be written by church members *before* the decisions are being made either in committee or on the floor of the house or senate.

I recall visiting Senator McGovern's office several years ago and discussing a certain bill relating to world hunger with his administrative assistant. The measure was due to come before the Foreign Relations Committee in a few days. "How is the mail coming in?" I asked. "Very light," he said. "We received two letters today and yours was one of them." Two billion dollars' worth of food and only two letters to the sponsor of the bill! Except on emotional issues (such as gun control, abortion, or the school prayer amendment), whatever mail the prophetic community generates from church people will have an impact out of proportion to its numbers. On most bills there is only a trickle of communications.

Register Citizen Opinion, an excellent resource for letter writers, offers guidelines on content, forms of address with proper mailing addresses, committee assignments, etc. (Available for 35 cents from the Board of Church and Society, 100 Maryland Avenue, N.E., Washington, D.C. 20002.)

Letters are a useful means of influencing public legislation. One staff member, with more than 20 years of service on Capitol Hill, said he thought that a half dozen letters from constituents, even though scrawled with pencil on brown wrapping paper, would be enough to change a representative's vote on most issues!

Telephoning is another effective means of communication, particularly if a vote is imminent. If your group cannot reach your representative or senator personally, leave a brief message with the secretary, who will transmit it as soon as possible.

Western Union provides a special rate for "Public Opinion Messages" of 15 words. These are especially useful when sent within a day or two of an anticipated vote. A large number of telegrams coming in from concerned persons in your church is likely to have a significant influence. Your political-action committee may wish to list and contact church members who would be willing to cooperate in such an effort. Be sure to let the senders phrase their messages in their own words.

Visiting Washington with a group from your church provides an exceptional opportunity to discuss issues directly with legislators. Just telephone the offices you wish to visit to set up appointments. (All offices can be reached through 202/CA 4-3121, the Capitol switchboard.) The prophetic community could set up such a trip and act as an enabler for the experience.

Visits to congressional hearings, to various embassies, to the State Department, the Agency for International Development, the Department of Housing and Urban Development, the Civil Rights Commission, the Department of Energy, and various national organization offices (Common Cause, SANE, AFL-CIO) can be an exciting part of such a trip and should shed light on important public issues. Then, when you go to see your representative and senators, you will be more adequately informed. In many cases, the Washington office of your denomination could arrange your schedule to meet your needs. The prophetic community may well find that such a Washington seminar will so enliven its church members that either their own membership or the support group will be increased.

Remember, there are times when your members of congress are back in their home districts—Easter, August, Christmas vacation, and an increasing number of long weekends growing out of the new policy of placing national holidays on Mondays or Fridays. These periods give representatives and senators an excellent chance to respond to the grass roots.

The first thing a congressperson reads in the morning is the newspaper from the home district. I remember visiting the late Senator Hubert Humphrey's office with a group on a disarmament issue. He had a book of local news clippings on a table beside his desk. The senator said that in odd moments between appointments he looked through these news items from Minnesota local papers to see what people were interested in back in the home state. Thus, the most important initial input into the thinking of a member of congress during a given day is what is read in a local daily or county weekly newspaper. Most such papers welcome articles and letters to the editor, and they are another means of communicating with your legislators. Try it. Most congresspersons want to get reelected.

With regard to timing, Christians who attempt to exercise responsible citizenship should keep in mind that about 90% of the bills passed by congress are adopted in virtually the same form in which they were reported out of committee. Thus, sending communications while the congressional committee is still meeting is important.

If your group's representative (or senator) is on the committee, so much the better. If not, writing directly to the chairperson of the committee is considered appropriate since that official is expected to be sensitive to the concerns of all Americans.

Every representative and senator has a vote; and if the tally on a bill is expected to be close, the way they vote may be crucial. Communicating with legislators after a bill is out of committee and before the vote on the house and senate floors is the next optimum time for influencing legislation.

Yes, the prophetic community can become involved effectively in the legislative process. It has done so in the past. Concerned Christians were an important part of the effort to establish an Arms Control and Disarmament Agency in 1961. They participated on an ecumenical basis in efforts to obtain a Civil Rights Bill in 1964. They were involved in passage of the omnibus Housing Bill in 1968.

And because the Disarmament Agency had been established early in the '60s, it was possible to have a trained corps of negotiators to implement the recent SALT talks on disarmament. Because of the 1964 civil rights measure, which set up the Equal Employment Opportunity Commission, it was possible later to provide the agency with enforcement powers in fair employment. As a result of the housing legislation of 1968, church groups were able to form housing corporations and help build homes for low- and moderate-income families. One decent act makes another possible.

The local political-action committee ought to see itself as part of a legislative network. It is quite possible that your denomination may have established some kind of network. Or possibly they may have a national legislative bulletin. Get on their mailing list. Also, the committee should consider joining IMPACT, a national legislative network operated by the religious community in Washington. IMPACT is organized in a number of legislative districts around the country with persons from churches and synagogues working together as they seek to exert a benevolent influence on their respective members of congress. IMPACT puts out various publications, including *Prepare, Up-Date,* and *Action.* For $7.50 you can join the IMPACT network by writing to this address: 110 Maryland Avenue, N.E., Washington, D.C. 20002.

How to Deal with Resistant Church Members

In many churches political action on issues will not be popular. It may seem to be divisive. On the other hand, it may bring people together around noble objectives. Surely it is important to have the pastor of the local church behind the church's public-policy initiatives. However, the pastor does not have to be on the action committee. If he or she opposes its work, that will make things difficult. The only other route would be to go interfaith or at least ecumenical.

There may be archconservatives, or even John Birchers, in a given church. The political-action committee will not please them—unless they control it. But it would be best not to look for trouble. In the beginning you may wish to support items that are apt to be least offensive, such as childcare legislation. Very few people are against the well-being of children.

Nevertheless, if the opposition objects to your activity, be gentle. They are children of God, too. Try to enter a dialogue with them. But don't give up simply because some people object to your procedures. Move ahead without being abrasive.

Should the local committee become connected with a political party or certain candidates? Actually, the advice of the Amsterdam Assembly of the World Council of Churches in 1948 was instructive at this point:

> The Church as such should not be identified with any political party, and it must not act as though it were itself a political party. In general, the formation of such parties is hazardous because they easily confuse Christianity with the inherent compromises of politics. They may cut off Christians from the other parties which need the leaven of Christianity, and they may consolidate all who do not share the political principles of the Christian party not only against that party but against Christianity itself.[9]

Nor would it be wise to support certain candidates officially, even if they belong to your church. This could be truly divisive and would not be worth the risk. Church members could be encouraged to perform this needful task through local party activity and other caucus groups which may be formed. The major focus for church persons will always be upon the issues, and especially upon those issues where values are at stake.

Should the Christian Church Be Involved in Lobbying at All?

There are some who would say that what I have just suggested is basically illegal since it represents engaging in lobbying and thus will cause trouble for the church. By "trouble," they mean, among other things, that the church could lose its tax-deductible status.

Such persons often do believe in social witness, social education, and social service—but they do not believe in political action.

Such people would see nothing improper, in a free society, for the highway lobby (cement, auto, and heavy machinery) to attempt to influence legislation to secure more highways and approval of wider, heavier trucks to ride on them. Also, the domestic sugar industry should not be denied the right to seek import quotas on sugar. The textile industry has the right to lobby for protection in the Trade Bill, and the cotton industry has the right to lobby for support prices for cotton. Whether they agreed with them or not, they would not prevent the National Rifle Association from trying to stop the enactment of gun-control legislation. They have that right to protect their interests. But the church should not exercise its power to protect its recognized ethical interests.

Those who believe the church should not lobby may oppose the products and services of the tobacco, alcohol, and gambling industries but they generally would not prevent them from pursuing their interests on Capitol Hill. This group often believes that the church is in a special category; it should place itself above the battle and not become involved in either politics or national issues. This position has something to do with the separation of the church and state, although this is often not defined. There is something unseemly, they contend, about the church's becoming involved in anything related to politics—like placing a stain on the holy vestments.

One further reason many of these people are against the church's relating to national issues is that this will, they feel, break the fellowship, split the church wide open, and destroy Christian unity which they value. Also, such action on controversial issues would hurt the income of the church.

These persons feel that church members should fulfill their citizenship responsibilities as individuals, becoming informed on the issues and writing to their congresspersons, and so on, on a purely personal basis. They feel that the church, as a church, should not take official positions on national issues, that the leaders of the church should not speak out on public questions or in any way appear to give the impression that they are representing the viewpoints of the millions in their constituency.

Those Who Feel the Church Should Lobby

Christians who support lobbying believe that the underlying concept of political action is valid: "Groups in our society should relate to policy-makers to effect change." One of these groups is the church.

They believe that the church, like other organizations and institutions, also has the right to attempt to preserve and advance its interests. They feel, however, that the church should not represent a narrow, self-serving, institutional interest but rather should promote the public interest. That is, the church, given its ethical precepts, should work on behalf of what seems to be right and good for all of God's children.

If the church decides to make Christianity as effective as possible in the life of the country, then, these people say, the church must relate meaningfully to the great national issues. Relating ethics to power is an essential factor in implementing social change. No institution is in a better position to do this than the church. The church is expressing its beliefs and having its effect even when it does nothing. Its silence and withdrawal gives tacit consent—just as the silence of the German church, except in rare instances such as Pastor Niemöller, gave consent to the rise of Nazi power.

Therefore, the church should exercise its moral responsibility. In the name of Christ who blessed the peacemakers, it should take positions on important international treaties—such as those on genocide and disarmament. In the name of a belief in the dignity and worth of human personality, the church should relate to a Voting Rights Bill and Equal Employment Opportunity legislation. In the name of those who have exalted "the perfect law of liberty" (as James put it), the church should seek to preserve civil liberties. In the name of Christ who engaged in a ministry of healing, the church should be concerned about national health legislation. With all of this, although education of the membership is extremely important, the leadership of the church has a special responsibility: the responsibility to serve as the *"advance conscience"* of the nation. In other words, the church, to be true to its tradition, must serve a *prophetic* as well as a pastoral function. The prophets of the Old Testament never took a Gallup poll before speaking out on an unpopular issue.

Now it is true that, if the church becomes a prophetic community in the arena of political action, there may be disagreement among the membership. There may be some who will fall away and the church could be fewer in numbers, but, at the same time, remaining members may be more loyal and devoted. In the first few hundred years the Christian church was a small, disciplined, and effective band. In A.D. 312, when Roman Emperor Constantine became converted and Christianity became the official religion, hordes of persons came into the church, and it was very popular. However, this period was quickly followed by a thousand years of Dark Ages and civilization almost perished. Would it not be better to have a smaller, more deeply dedicated church, indeed, a prophetic community, seeking to apply Christianity in every area of life than a larger church where the popular culture has so invaded the church that it stands for nothing distinctive to the outsider and is afraid to act lest some "insider" might object?

Courage, brothers and sisters!

7.

THE PROPHETIC COMMUNITY AND INTERNATIONAL AFFAIRS

In 1964 after the Civil Rights Bill had passed the congress, Senator Richard Russell, leader of the opposition, was interviewed by the press on the Capitol steps. They asked him how he accounted for his defeat. He responded: "The churches supported the bill."

I suspect that if SALT III or any other genuine disarmament proposal is successfully adopted by our nation it will be because the spiritual and moral force exerted by the churches provided effective motivation in the direction of world peace.

Only the churches will be able to propel our people toward a world where:

—reconciliation rather than nuclear vengeance keeps nations from war;

—spiritual security replaces a security based on the threat of nuclear overkill;

—"the builders outstrip the destroyers."

Why, then, doesn't the church get on with the job?

Why the Church Has Ignored World Peace

The church has had a terrible problem in relating to the issues of world peace. This is true for several reasons. World peace is far away and the way church people have traditionally dealt with it is to support missionary projects. No one would contend that many of these projects—particularly those which have included the concerns of health, education, and agricultural development—have not created goodwill in the less developed world. However, historically speaking, it has not been the developing nations, but the great powers, that have fought the most devastating conflicts. We haven't yet learned how to relate effectively to the great powers, particularly the Soviet Union.

Another problem for church people has been that to suggest policies or programs that would promote peace with the Russians has meant being the object of accusations of "pro-communism." No one really likes to be accused of being "pro-communist," so this has served as a handicap to improved relations between the superpowers, the Soviet Union and the United States.

Thirdly, foreign policy questions are tremendously complicated and, therefore, Christians tend to be frightened away from dealing with them. It is much more comfortable to say "we don't know enough" or "let us trust our leaders" in this sphere.

Among Christian bodies, only the Quakers have used the full force of their spiritual strength to pursue the paths of peace and to become heavily involved in the areas of foreign policy, disarmament, the United Nations, development, etc. And even in this case, it must be admitted that the American Friends Service Committee was awarded the Nobel Peace Prize largely because of its *relief* work following World War II.

Most mainline churches do not bring the peace agenda into the programs of their local congregations. Therefore, it has been more difficult to find model projects for this volume in the area of world peace than in any other field. The author would have to conclude that this is largely due to the difficulty of relating meaningfully to international relations that has inhibited the churches from becoming involved. A lot of churches do "study" the problems of peace. But not many do anything about it. Studying serious international questions is, however, very important.

One could conclude that if our nation had an overwhelming will to world peace, working out the details would fall into place. Time and time again, responsible polls in our nation have shown that Americans support the United Nations, favor human rights, would pursue disarmament efforts, and feel positive about foreign aid. Yet the depth of that commitment can be questioned. Americans also think of the United Nations as a "debating society," willingly support generous arms to dictatorships, are anxious about the United States being inferior to the Russians in any weapons category, and favor chopping off foreign aid with a meat axe every time our economy hits a slump.

The Church's Peace Concern

So there is a job to be done by the churches in helping to secure a deeper commitment to the fundamental components of a peaceful world. There was a time when that commitment became evident. During World War II, through the church's Commission on a Just and Durable Peace, local congregations educated their members in preparation for the establishment of the United Nations after the war. John Foster Dulles, who headed that commission, spoke about this in an address at the Washington Cathedral on March 11, 1948:

> Internationally and nationally, the churches have organized themselves to put the impress of Christian thinking upon the life of nations. That effort is already showing positive results.
>
> It was the Christian churches of America that in 1941 took the initiative in demanding that, after the war, there should be a world organization in which the United States would participate. That peace aim had been omitted from the Atlantic Charter because President Roosevelt and Prime Minister Churchill feared that the prevalent American mood was still that which 20 years before had rejected the League of Nations. Whether or not they were right at the moment, they were not right for long. The churches saw to that. They conducted intensively throughout this land national missions and study groups on world order, with the result that our political leaders knew they were following the popular will when, two years after the Atlantic Charter, they made world organization an added peace objective.[10]

The churches could effectively educate for peace again if they so determined. Surely the peace emphasis of a local church should be more than simply having a missionary speaker once a year and sending the children out on the UNICEF drive, admirable as these may be in themselves.

The Christian church has no right to be proud of the barbarous Crusades of the twelfth century or of the bloody religious wars of the sixteenth century. But the church has come a long way since it sold war bonds from the pulpit during World War I. Within the mainline churches there is a genuine peace concern as evidenced by official policy positions. But these seldom are reflected in the programs or projects of local churches. Yet scattered here and there are peace projects that are significant and remarkable.

Scriptural Motivation for Peace

Surely there is sound reason found in Holy Scriptures for Christian motivation to become a prophetic community actively working on behalf of world peace. Had it not been that Christ lived in an era of *Pax Romana,* an enforced peace, it is quite likely that he would have spoken more forcefully on this subject. Nevertheless, the Gospels do hold up the ideals of peace.

Heralding Christ's coming, the Scripture records that angels cried out the meaning of his birth: "Glory to God in the highest, and on earth peace among men. . . . " (Luke 2:14) And during the last week of Jesus' life, as he drew near to Jerusalem, he wept over it, saying: "Would that even today you knew the things that make for peace!" (Luke 19:42) And in between, during his ministry, his message was clear. For in the introduction of the Sermon on the Mount, the Prophet of Nazareth proclaimed: "Blessed are the peacemakers, for they shall be called sons of God." (Matt. 5:9)

Jesus' followers understood his focus on peace and Saint Paul said in the famous twelfth chapter of Romans: "If possible, so far as it depends upon you, live peaceably with all." (Rom. 12:18) And the author of 1 Peter wrote:

> "He that would love life
> and see good days . . .
> let him seek peace and pursue it.
> For the eyes of the Lord are
>   upon the righteous,
> and his ears are open to their prayer."
>   [1 Pet. 3:10-12]

Although much of what Christ and his followers said about "peace" applied to individuals, it also may and should apply to the realm of international affairs. For our job is not just to mimic Jesus but to translate his spirit in such a way that it bears meaningfully upon our total society, including the international scene.

Organizing for Peace

Churches that have developed serious programs of Bible study will be motivated to do something that contributes to world peace. But many will feel uneducated. This being the case, the Peace Committee of the local church or Social Concerns Commission must educate within the membership. An assessment of local resources will need to be made. Are there returned missionaries? professors of international relations? persons who have been in the Peace Corps or served with the Agency for International Development? Are there peace organizations or foreign affairs councils or United Nations Associations within the reach of the local church?

The persons enumerated above could serve on the church World Peace Committee, or at least be resources for educational forums or discussions with existing church groups. If your church is medium-sized, it may be able to sustain a World Peace Committee or a subcommittee of Social Concerns. Other persons who might make good committee members are students who have majored in international relations, young people or adults with overseas or world travel experience, foreign students temporarily residing in the community, persons who belong to peace-oriented groups, such as the Fellowship of Reconciliation, World Federalists, New Directions, or the United Nations Association.

One excellent study which any church or its adult church school class might undertake is the annual "Great Decisions" discussions offered by the Foreign Policy Association. Forums are often held each year in the community or on television or radio which could serve as background material. If you have trouble securing study books locally, they can be obtained from the Foreign Policy Association, 345 East 46th Street, New York, New York 10017. Also, church groups may wish to order study guides prepared by the Council on Religion and International Affairs. These supplements explore ethical and religious values in relation to the eight topics selected for the year. CRIA Supplements can be ordered for 40 cents each from CRIA, 170 East 64th Street, New York, New York 10021.

Whatever is done, the World Peace Committee, if it would seek to help the church become a truly prophetic community in international affairs, has a tough assignment. For it means helping people here in the United States to feel the hurt afflicting others elsewhere. It means being touched by those we cannot touch in our everyday lives. It could mean being thought of as unpatriotic or communist by some persons—simply because we may question a huge U.S. military budget or because we sincerely want peace with the Russians. It also may mean being frustrated by armed conflicts and revolutions breaking out in faraway places where we seem to have little influence or control. Thus, it is very important that we find some handles and pursue some projects where modest success is measurable.

The Advance Issues

The World Peace Committee, or Committee on International Relations, will need to decide where it is going. This certainly means being able to delineate the key advance issues on which work could be done and then choosing among them for a concentration of efforts. Let me suggest a few of them:

World Hunger. There are still a depressing number of human beings facing stark hunger on our planet. Half of all children in the Third World are underfed. Twenty-two million babies born each year weigh less than five pounds at birth. More than 95% of these are in the developing countries.

Many countries of the developing world face draught, flood, and pestilence periodically and in those times are very short on food. At the same time, there are a number of nations which hover between producing surplus grain supplies or just enough to satisfy their own needs. In the short run, we need to be able to level out fluctuations in supply and meet periodic shortages through grain reserves and food aid. In the long run, many developing countries will have to improve and increase their own level of agricultural production. Over the long haul, we need to be able to move away from the present system, which tries to solve food shortages by shipping commodities from surplus areas to distant deficit countries.

Land for increasing food production is available in the Third World. Dr. Moise Mensah, a food production expert, states that only 15% of the arable land in South America, 20% in Africa, and 28% in Asia is now being used for agricultural production. But it may cost a lot of money to put these lands into production. The Overseas Economic Cooperation Fund of Japan has estimated that it would cost $67 billion to double rice production in Asia over the next 15 years.

Some persons are saying that self-sufficiency of the periodically hungry people is not necessarily the answer. Dr. Fred H. Sanderson of the Brookings Institution has said that in some cases poor countries could better feed themselves by exporting products in which they have a comparative advantage because of climate or inexpensive labor. Then they could use some of their export earnings to pay for grain imports.

Sometimes, we have congratulated ourselves because certain developing countries have increased economic growth when it really meant that the wealthy were getting richer and the poor were remaining in their poverty. Dr. Nevin Scrimshaw, Professor of Nutrition and Food Science at M.I.T., has suggested that instead of concentrating on improved yields for export from crop production on farmlands held by wealthy landowners, efforts should be made to increase yields on small farms producing for internal consumption. This, says Dr. Scrimshaw, would lead to nutritional improvement for the rural poor.

Among the developing nations, malnutrition occurs most seriously, says Dr. Scrimshaw, in pregnant or lactating mothers whose diets are not adequate to promote healthy fetal growth and development or to sustain proper growth of the newborn infant. The result is significantly higher mortality rates among infants in the developing countries as well as impaired mental and physical development.[11]

Disarmament. Writing in *World Military and Social Expenditures 1978,* Ruth Leger Sivard reported:

> *World military spending* went from $200 billion in 1970 to the current $400 billion. After allowance for price inflation, this meant

that yearly outlays had risen 15 per cent above the 1970 level, 60 per cent above 1960. Instead of the disarmament dividend expected at the end of the Vietnam War, the world arms budget had gone higher still.

Armed forces (regulars) increased to 23 million, about 2 million more than in 1970 and 7 million than in 1960. Comparable increases in para-military forces brought active military personnel to a total of 36 million.

Exports of major weapons to third world countries reached an estimated $8 billion yearly in constant 1975 prices, almost three times such exports in 1970, over four times volume in 1960.

Strategic nuclear stockpiles of the two super-powers rose to 14,000 warheads, an increase of 8,000 since 1970. There are also 500 or more deliverable nuclear weapons among other nuclear weapon states, which now include United Kingdom, France, China, India, and perhaps Israel. The explosive force of these stockpiles is equivalent to several tons of TNT for every person on earth.[12]

It is indeed a sobering thought that the combined explosive power of the nuclear weapons which the U.S. and the Soviet Union are aiming at each other's cities and military targets is 7,000 times that of all the bombs exploded in World War II. The idea behind all this power, at least on our side, is that it is possible, even if our country were hit by an all-out "first strike" coming from the Soviet Union, we could effectively retaliate with a "second strike" that would inflict unacceptable damage. *It is a bit disconcerting to Christians that our policy seems to be fundamentally based on assured vengeance.*

At the time this is being written a SALT II treaty is being discussed in the country. This treaty, if enacted, would basically put a lid on the development of strategic nuclear vehicles. It would set that limit at 2,400 for each country with a reduction of 2,250 before 1985. There would also be limits set on land-based intercontinental ballistic missiles and on submarine-launched ballistic missiles.[13]

If this treaty comes into force, then the movement would be toward an agreement on SALT III, which would meaningfully begin to provide for mutually safeguarded disarmament.

Many Americans wonder if the Russians can be trusted to actually implement any treaty they have signed. Actually, reliable verification of Soviet arms activity is possible through diverse and sophisticated intelligence techniques applied from adjacent land areas or submarines strategically located or monitors operating from space vehicles ("spy in the sky").

It is important as progress toward disarmament is attempted that treaties be agreed upon which will be mutually advantageous. Any treaty between the United States and the Soviet Union which favors one side will probably be broken. On the other hand, we are well aware that the most damaging inflationary factor in the American economy has been arms expenditures. We are also aware that huge military budgets in the U.S.S.R. have kept the Russians from enjoying the consumption of otherwise more plentiful consumer goods. Disarmament and peace are advantageous on both sides.

One of the serious blocks to disarmament in the United States has been the difficulty of moving away from communities that must depend upon arms factories and installations toward cities and towns whose economies are focused on peaceful pursuits. The president has recently recommended that dozens of army bases around the country be eliminated. As usual, this causes a furor out in the congressional districts and certain powerful members of congress will be able to turn back this recommendation in their own areas. We Americans have a great fear of peace because we have become so dependent upon war jobs for our existence.

A man of great insight and compassion, Walter Reuther of the United Automobile Workers, once said: "I think it is a terrible thing for a human being to feel that his security and the well-being of his family hinge upon a continuation of the insanity of the arms race. We have to give these people greater economic security in terms of the rewarding purposes of peace."[14]

The trouble with a war economy is that it doesn't really help the nation to the extent we've been led to think. In fact, military spending creates fewer jobs than most civilian spending—largely because it is very capital intensive. Military spending accelerates inflation. In the case of weapons expenditures themselves, it often means substantial dollars chasing nonconsumable goods. You can't eat a bomb and most weapons soon become obsolete—so the usable assets of the nation have been depleted and productive labor has been expended on nonconsumable products. Because a disproportionate share of our nation's wealth has been diverted to war production, there have been insufficient funds left to meet the desperate needs of the nation for improving education, sustaining health, and overcoming poverty.

If your local church group would like some help in planning to convert an army base or an arms industry in your area to peaceful uses and at the same time preserve jobs, you may wish to subscribe to "The Conversion Planner" put out by SANE, 318 Massachusetts Avenue, N.E., Washington, D.C. 20002.

At this writing it is impossible to know if SALT II will be ratified by the U.S. Senate. Assuming that it will, there is no question that SALT III will represent a very challenging objective. The reason for this is that this treaty will be the first agreement where *actual* disarmament will begin to take place. And for that reason it will be essential that churches participate in the discussions and contemplated action. SALT I put a lid on nuclear weapons; SALT II was designed to do the same thing with nuclear delivery vehicles, that is, missiles. But SALT III's purpose will be to initiate the reduction process. Stability and security in the past have meant equality at a higher level. However, security can also be achieved at a lower level.

In the name of one who said "Blessed are the peacemakers," the churches should plan to get into the debate on SALT III early. When the time comes, an excellent source for current information would be: The Coalition for a New Foreign and Military Policy, 120 Maryland Avenue, N.E., Washington, D.C. 20002.

Human Rights. Jesus brought dignity to the persons with whom he related: women, the poor, foreigners, the ostracized. The dignity of human beings is disavowed when they are denied the right to worship as they please, when they are cast into prison for political beliefs, when they are exploited by their rulers, when they are tortured by dictators.

To be fully Christian means to be free—to worship God, to read the Scriptures, to speak out against injustice, and to work unhampered for a better human society. Fences, prisons, muzzles, chains, whips, and electric prods are alien equipment to the Christian.

The whole area of human rights promises to be one that begs for attention from sensitive and conscientious Christians. In most of the world, populations live under regimes that cannot be fairly judged as free—the communist world, most of Southeast Asia, most of Latin America, and South Africa come painfully to mind. Democratic nations are in a distinct minority. How do we relate to nonfree peoples in the future? Do we go to war to liberate them? Probably not, because that would violate another principle we hold dear, the right of nonintervention. Do we raise such a fuss that we alienate other countries whose goodwill we cherish—such as the Soviet Union? Do we foment civil war or seek to overturn authoritarian regimes surreptitiously?

Very few answers are incontrovertibly attractive except to set a good example and hold up the ideal. There is surely more opportunity to do that then we have inclination to pursue. When the Universal Declaration of Human Rights was adopted in 1948, it was upheld as "a universal standard for achievement"—a sort of plumbline by which nations were to measure themselves.

We certainly ought to keep holding that plumbline up to ourselves in the United States. At this writing the Genocide Convention, adopted by the United Nations in 1948, continues to languish in the U.S. Senate awaiting ratification more than thirty years later. Several other human rights treaties have been placed on the U.S. agenda for action—those on racial discrimination, economic, social, and cultural rights, and civil and political rights.

The United States will need to consider over the next several years whether it is setting as good an example for the world as it might in terms of domestic social and economic rights. For one is not fully free if one can enter the election booth, but not the job market; if one has the right to check into any hotel, but not the funds to check out at the grocery counter; if one can vote for the coroner, but can't get the medical care that will extend life.

As an advance issue, human rights, unfortunately, is likely to wear well. The Christian is obligated to be involved. One resource that might be useful to church committees would be Amnesty International, U.S.A., 2112 Broadway, New York, New York 10023.

Strengthening the United Nations. Even church people become disturbed occasionally by the way the United Nations operates. We sometimes see it as "only a debating society." We see the Third World nations outvoting the more economically and militarily powerful developed nations in the General Assembly. We see the communist nations using the U.S. as a podium for propaganda. We hear criticisms of the United Nations and its agencies being overstaffed and overpaid. We saw black Africa in the U.N. restrained in its criticism of dictator Idi Amin of Uganda while hypercritical of democratically elected Bishop Muzorewa of Zimbabwe-Rhodesia. We view the U.N. as seeming powerless to do anything about Vietnam pushing its "boat people" out to sea. We see the Third World countries in the United Nations much more critical of the United States as a major oil-consuming country than they are of O.P.E.C. nations, even though advancing oil prices hurt them proportionately more than the developed world.

But we must bear all this. For such is the role of a great power—to be objective and willing to absorb even unjust criticism.

Regardless, it is in the interests of the United States and the members of our churches to support and strengthen the United Nations. We were there at its creation. Church representatives were present in a meaningful way at the San Francisco constituting assembly in 1945. They had a major part in seeing that one of the four purposes of the U.N. was given a prominent place in the Charter—"to reaffirm faith in fundamental human rights. . . . " John Foster Dulles, U.S. representative to the San Francisco conference, had been chairman for several years of the Federal Council of Churches' Commission on a Just and Durable Peace.

Christians accept the counsel of Paul: "If possible, so far as it depends upon you, live peaceably with all." (Rom. 12:18) It is well applied to nations as well as to individuals. Christian churches which have adopted a "peacemaker" role know that the United Nations is an essential international instrument. As has so often been said: "If there were no U.N., we'd have to create one." But there *is* a United Nations. It is important because it is always better to talk than to fight—especially in a world armed with nuclear weapons. It is hard to imagine that the less developed countries could have achieved an annual growth rate of 5% a year without the help of the U.N. Development Program. It is impossible to imagine that malaria could have been eradicated without the ministrations of the World Health Organization. It is unlikely that the Cuban Missile Crisis of 1962 ever would have been averted if the United Nations Security Council had not been called upon for help. No one can bear to contemplate what the plight of children around the world might be without UNICEF acting as their agent.

While this is being written, U.N. delegates are gathered together for a Law of the Sea Conference at Geneva. If they agree upon a treaty and are able to establish a Seabed Authority, it will be the first time in history that the nations of the world will have given the United Nations some sovereignty over which to exercise authority. True, their sovereignty would extend only over the largely uninhabited five-sevenths of the world that is the ocean. But if our world is ever to come under the rule of law, there has to be a beginning. Christian churches, in the decade ahead, can encourage the establishment of world peace through world law.

Church groups which feel that "strengthening the United Nations" is a worthwhile advance issue to which they want to give some time will find it helpful to contact their local United Nations Association. Also, you could write to the national headquarters for information: United Nations Association, 300 East 42nd Street, New York, New York 10017.

To keep informed on the work of the United Nations and support its efforts, in 1962 there was established a Church Center for the United Nations. The thirteen-story structure is located directly across the street from the diplomatic entrance of the U.N. Church international affairs agencies are among its principal tenants. Thus, those church peace committees that wish to relate effectively to the U.N. can use this building as a resource. Its address is Church Center for the U.N., 777 United Nations Plaza, New York, New York 10017.

§

Only a few "advance issues" have been outlined in this chapter. A number of other international questions could be worthy of attention. Such might include: international development, population explosion, underground test ban treaty, permanent U.N. peacekeeping force, nuclear proliferation, United Nations Charter revision, international economic order, free trade, and international environmental protection.

Peace Action Projects

World Peacemakers. On a Sunday in the spring of 1979, a group from a small church in Washington, D.C. initiated a two-day conference on world peace and disarmament at the First Baptist Church, the president's church. The Reverend William Sloane Coffin of Riverside Church, New York City, was one of the speakers and delivered the sermon at the morning worship service. The president was sitting in the pews.

What an imaginative way of trying to impact U.S. foreign policy! The name of the group is World Peacemakers and the name of the sponsoring church is the Church of the Saviour. That church truly is a *small* church with approximately 125 members. Yet it is a very influential church because it has consistently implemented a program of meaningful service and outreach.

World Peacemakers includes a program that any churches in the country could participate in—if they, indeed, have the will. One of the initiators was Gordon Cosby, pastor of the Church of the Saviour. In setting forth the philosophy of the organization, he declared:

> We are enabled by the Spirit to see the vision of a world that has abolished the war system, and empowered to respond to this vision in call. This vision, which is just one aspect of the Kingdom of God, provides us with a whole new understanding of reality. We are now freed from the conventional wisdom which views the arms race as an unquestionable necessity for our nation's security. The basis of our hope and security is the realization that this vision is in complete attunement with the Kingdom of God, and the will of God. With this new way of viewing reality, we soon realize that *the nuclear arms race is the overarching idolatry of our time.*

As Richard J. Barnet, president of World Peacemakers, explains, the group's program is based on an attempt to reverse the arms race. Therefore, he calls for the United States to:

—cease all nuclear weapons tests everywhere.

—cease all flight tests of missiles, military aircraft, and other nuclear weapons delivery vehicles.

—suspend for three years all plans to acquire new nuclear weapons systems.

—establish a National Commission on Conversion to convert military facilities and jobs to peaceful production.

In addition, he asks that "the United States pledge to work for the outlawing of nuclear weapons, *which are at least as barbarous as chemical and biological weapons now banned by international agreement*" (italics ours).

World Peacemakers promotes an in-depth understanding of what security means and how to achieve it in the near future. It focuses attention on the ethical, spiritual, economic, and political dimensions of disarmament and their interrelationship. It attempts to increase public understanding of the unique opportunities and the unprecedented dangers facing human-kind. The organization presents the urgent need and possibilities for the United States to take bold action in stopping the arms race.

The Peacemakers program seeks to establish new Peacemaker groups. Such groups are to be committed to both an inward and an outward journey. The inward journey means seeking the genuine basis for true security in Christ. Groups would attempt to grow together in their inward life through prayer, reflection, and contemplation. The inward journey is to flow naturally to an outward journey of peacemaking. Each group would decide on its own strategies. But it is suggested that each Peacemaker write letters to friends and relatives raising the issue of the arms race and encouraging them also to send letters to friends.

Considerable literature has been generated by World Peacemakers. Much of this is on the arms race and the movement toward "true security." One of the pieces distributed is called "Abolition, 1975-1985." It calls for "a citizens' movement firmly based on moral and ethical principles to work for the elimination of the war system, just as the institution of slavery was abolished."

World Peacemakers is dissatisfied with our nation's security being based on a "mass hostage system," on the threat to commit mass murder of innocent people. Dr. Richard Barnet throws out the challenge to Christians: "Is it possible for the church to play a prophetic role at this critical moment in human history by launching a massive public education campaign to help the American people to confront the moral bankruptcy of the policies and institutions that are providing them with the illusion of security at the cost of sacrificing their most precious beliefs?"

World Peacemakers believes the church can. Many social action committees in local churches around the country will want to confirm that faith. You can find out more about the organization by writing to: World Peacemakers, 2852 Ontario Road, N.W., Washington, D.C. 20009. (See page 180.) The material on which this section is based came from literature published by World Peacemakers.

Foreign Student Weekend. Another project local churches of most any size could engage in would be a "Foreign Student Weekend."

I have been involved in these projects with the congregations of two churches where I served as pastor. One was a small town in exurban Chicago. Another was in a county-seat town in northern Illinois. Fundamentally, what you are trying to do in this peace-action program is to promote international understanding and goodwill through bringing your congregation in touch with some able respresentatives of countries around the world.

The host church needs to be in the reasonable vicinity of a university or college where there are a number of overseas students in attendance. The contact might well be made through the college's Christian Student Association, Wesley Foundation, Westminster Foundation, etc. In any event, one of the Christian student centers on campus would probably be willing to cooperate in contacting the students and checking to see if they are available for Saturday or Sunday on specific dates. Date selection is quite important since it is necessary to pick a time when students are likely to be available without interfering with exam schedules. Also, some of the weekend should be kept free so they can manage their assignments. About six or eight students would make a good group for adequate variety.

The students might be picked up for the weekend, for example, on late Saturday afternoon and brought to the church. From there, their "host families" would take them to their homes for dinner and for getting acquainted with their own families. In many cases, this is the first time a church family has ever had any direct and personal encounter with a person (or persons) from, say, Columbia, Brazil, Nigeria, Egypt, India, Indonesia, or the Philippine Islands. Often they will recall their encounter with fondness as their guest's country is in the news in years to come. It usually works out better if young people are a part of a host family.

What the church does to make the best use of the Foreign Student Weekend is entirely up to the determination of the planning committee. However, some churches have found it well to use the students' talents in the church's Sunday program. For example, at least some of the students might well be used to speak to various departments of the church school. This could be a rare treat for many of the pupils. Also, it is possible that some of the foreign students could participate in the Sunday morning church service. In case there is a graduate student in the group with sufficient religious background, it might be possible for such a person to deliver a meaningful and inspirational sermon related to world peace or international understanding.

The visiting students may return to their church member hosts for Sunday dinner or be shared with another family in the church. In the midafternoon, it may be possible to gather the students together with the young people of the church and form a panel for discussion purposes on "What Can Be Done to Promote World Peace." After the discussion, there could be a recreation period with folk dances of various countries being highlighted. Guests might be asked to share one of their own games with the youth for mutual enjoyment.

The evening concludes with an "International Supper" in which food representing specialty dishes from various countries is served. Fond farewells and pledges of renewed friendship close the evening. Arrangements should be made to return the students to their college residences by about eight o'clock so they can complete any study assignments remaining. Anyone wishing further information about the Foreign Student Weekend may write to the author: J. Elliott Corbett, 100 Maryland Avenue, N. E., Washington, D. C. 20002.

UNICEF Drive. A UNICEF drive in the local church and community may not be very dramatic, but it is meaningful in permitting Christians to relate in a useful way to developing countries and their needs—especially the needs of children and mothers.

For example, in 1978 UNICEF:

> —supplied vaccines and medicines for tuberculosis, diptheria, pertussis, tetanus, measles, polio, malaria, leprosy and trachoma to protect and treat millions of children.
>
> —provided technical supplies and equipment for 40,700 health centers of various kinds—hospitals, urban and rural health centers.
>
> —assisted programs to supply clean water and improved sanitation in 77 countries. Some 8.7 million people (roughly 45 percent of them children) benefited from over 28,500 pure water supply systems.
>
> Assistance to maternal and child health, including an expanded program of immunization, is the largest single field of UNICEF activity (amounting to nearly 52 percent of its total assistance). In 1978 UNICEF spent $74.7 million for health programs, including water supply, in 103 countries.[15]

In a discussion with Lloyd Bailey, Executive Secretary for the U.S. Committee for UNICEF, not long ago, he said the churches had been prime sponsors of the annual UNICEF drive at Halloween. Most churches that have participated have found much enjoyment and reward in taking part.

Materials should be ordered from the U.S. Committee for UNICEF well in advance—at least by early September. Perhaps only one church in the community or neighborhood will take part or, better yet, it can be an ecumenical project. The children of the church should be well prepared for participation. The occasion can be an excellent educational opportunity to enlighten the children and the whole church as to the positive aspects of United Nations programs. A film on the work of UNICEF might be shown in the church school on a preceding Sunday.

The Committee on Education of the church may wish to be involved in the selection of an optimum date for the UNICEF drive itself. Often the

Sunday afternoon before Halloween is a good time. It can be done while it is still light out so parents monitoring the event in automobiles can keep better watch over the children. Or, in this era of energy conservation, parents could walk with groups of children and hover nearby as the appeal is made.

A little party of cocoa and cookies and a few games may be worked out by the women of the church with the youth assisting. To order materials and receive other useful information, write to: U.S. Committee for UNICEF, 331 East 38th Street, New York, New York 10016. (See page 180.)

United Nations Seminar. One project which any church or small group of churches can implement is a United Nations Seminar. It is possible to gather a group of interested church members together—youth or adults—for a trip to the United Nations headquarters in New York City in order to promote international understanding and peace. One could say that such a trip is purely educational. Not so. It is possible at the U.N. to visit with the U.S. Mission to the U.N., with various U.N. staff persons, with agency personnel, with U.N. missions of other countries, and raise questions and, to a limited extent, exert influence.

If a group from a local church is to visit the United Nations, they ought first to spend a number of months studying that international organization so as to secure the most advantage from the trip. Current issues especially should be reviewed by seminar participants. A group can profit from such a stimulating experience only if sufficient background study is engaged in. Materials can be ordered from your denominational international affairs office and from the U.N. Information Office in your region. Certainly studies should be implemented in the fields of disarmament, international development, strengthening the United Nations, Law of the Sea, and human rights. (See page 179.)

Most local groups can arrange to rent a bus or travel in a caravan of vans. If as far away as the Rocky Mountains or the West Coast, air travel should be considered. Fund-raising activities and some subsidy from the church should be given consideration perhaps a year in advance of the scheduled trip.

The trip should be fun and include some sightseeing and theater attendance, but the focal point of the seminar should not be lost—better understanding of the major world peacemaking body, the United Nations and its agencies.

While in New York be sure to spend time at the Church Center for the United Nations, across the street from the main U.N. entrance. There, church agencies will be glad to host your group and provide their on-the-spot know-how to make your U.N. visit more meaningful. Also, plan to visit a session of the General Assembly or one of the Councils of the United Nations. Your international affairs office will help you secure tickets for admission. The general tour of the U.N. building is also an impressive experience. You may be able to arrange for lunch in the U.N. delegates' diningroom. In any case, in addition to contacts with your denominational office for help with planning your seminar program and setting up your schedule, write to: Seminars on National and International Affairs, 777 United Nations Plaza, Room 800, New York, New York 10017.

Infant Formula Action Project. Those churches willing to take on a project with some clout in it may wish to consider the Nestlé boycott. Just as many Christians support positive work being accomplished in developing countries, such as UNICEF, they also oppose operations in the Third World which harm children. A number of churches from the local to the national level have joined the Nestlé boycott. They do so out of conscience. It is interesting to note that the focal point for the movement, Infant Formula Action Coalition (INFACT), is located at the Catholic student headquarters—the Newman Center at the University of Minnesota. Both Catholic and Protestant groups, however, are in support of the project.

As INFACT literature points out, the concern centers around the fact that millions of Third World babies are starving because of the distribution there of infant formula by Nestlé and other multinational corporations. The eyes of these babies are sunken, their bellies are swollen, their arms and legs are like sticks. They have diarrhea.

Perhaps it is best to let Dr. Benjamin Spock, the famed baby doctor, describe the concern in his own words:

> Nestlé, the largest food processor in the world, is actively encouraging mothers in the developing countries in Africa, Asia and South America to give up breast feeding and turn to powdered milk formula instead.
> But in such countries water is contaminated, sterilization procedures are unknown, illiteracy makes proper preparation impossible, and poor people try to stretch the powered milk supply by over-diluting their baby's formula.
> The tragic results are widespread malnutrition and severe infant diarrhea that often ends in death.
> Despite worldwide protest Nestlé continues to put profits first and refuses to halt this traffic with death.
> So we are trying, by boycott, to compel Nestlé to do what they won't do out of decency.

Douglas Johnson, chairperson of INFACT, tells what happens specifically to the new mothers in the Third World who become sold on the use of infant formula:

> Throughout the Third World, from Haiti to Venezuela, from Nigeria to the Philippines, new mothers are leaving maternity wards with tins of powdered infant formula—free samples supplied by companies based in the U.S., Japan, and Switzerland.

They go home. They open the tins. They try to reconstitute the formula. Without clean water. Without a suitable pot for sterilization. Without enough fuel to boil their one bottle and nipple before each feeding. Without a refrigerator to store even a single day's supply of formula.

Their free tin runs out. Their breast milk by now has dried up. Now they *must* use the formula. But when they discover that it costs nearly half of all the money their families earn, they try to stretch it. They thin it down with water, tea, cocoa, to make a three-day supply last a week, two weeks, even three.

Soon their babies burn with fever. They suffer from dehydration and acute diarrhea. They are weakened by lack of nourishment, infected by poisonous bacteria, susceptible to disease.

Often these babies die. Information about the hazards of infant formula use has often come from church missisonaries operating in developing countries. The problem has been that certain internationally operating food companies have pushed the use of baby formula aggressively in the Third World. The babies would be much healthier sticking with breast feeding. Some of the companies previously engaging in this practice have stopped or modified their campaigns. But Nestlé has not. Hence the boycott has been directed against this single multi-national corporation based in Switzerland. Nestlé has defended itself by saying that they would be willing to abide by the decision of an impartial World Health Organization Conference called especially to deal with this question. Such a conference has been held, but its recommendations have been variously interpreted. Meanwhile, the formula continues to be distributed and babies continue to die.

The Nestié Corporation sells such diverse products as Nescafé, Souptime, Taster's Choice, Libby's, and Stouffer's labeled foods as well as candy bars. Thus, church people are being requested to participate in the boycott. Your church may wish to join in the boycott if the question is not settled by the time you read this. Material on which this section is based was obtained from INFACT. For further information, write to INFACT, 1701 University Avenue, S. E., Minneapolis, Minnesota 55414. If you would like to secure the Nestlé Corporation point of view, write to: Nestlé Co., Inc., 100 Bloomingdale Road, White Plains, New York 10605.

Educating for Peace Action. There isn't a church alive that cannot educate for peace and then expect that such education will lead to some kind of personal political action. One church that actually did this was the Central United Methodist Church of Stockton, California.

Fundamentally, the pastor, Dr. Robert W. Moon, preached four sermons on world peace in January of 1978. These were on the theme of "Beating Our Swords into Plowshares" and treated the subjects of "The Risks We Face," "The Myths that Enslave Us," "Far-out Peace Ideas," and "A Far Better Way." Following each sermon, there were discussion groups in the fellowship hall which were led by able and trained persons. Immediately following the last session, a time was provided for raising questions with the pastor.

Several months later one of the adult classes spent six weeks discussing related issues under professional leadership. The pastor, Dr. Moon, states that "many letters were written to the president, the Secretary of State, and our congresspersons and senators."

The Central United Methodist Church has prepared a booklet on the peace education program, including the sermons, discussion questions, biblical references, a bibliography, and thirteen ideas on "What One Person Can Do." Both the pamphlet and the sermons are an excellent peace education and action source. Toward the conclusion of the resource, a quote is provided from former President Dwight D. Eisenhower. It says:

> I like to believe that people, in the long run, are going to do more to promote peace than governments. Indeed, I think the people want peace so much that one of these days governments had better get out of the way and let them have it.

Just previous to the presentation of the "peace action suggestions," the Swords into Plowshares pamphlet states that "churches and church people have a responsibility to help create the atmosphere in this nation and in the world that will make it possible for the leaders of the nations to do what they ought to do."

That is very true. If you would like to secure a copy of "Beating Our Swords into Plowshares" with the idea of using it as a resource in your local church, send one dollar to the Central United Methodist Church, 3700 Pacific Avenue, Stockton, California 95204.

A possible variation of such a program might be to use the current "Great Decisions" study (see p. 79) in your local church and make a determination in advance that the studies will lead to some action by the group. Often these studies deal in a concise and helpful way with the critical international issues facing the nation. I gratefully acknowledge that I first learned about the Vietnam war in an authoritative way by reading about its existence and the agonizing choices we were making as explained in a Great Decisions booklet.

Studies in the 1979 Great Decisions program included chapters on Technology and World Development, Dealing with China, Black Africa, and World Law of the Oceans.

Investing for Peace. Some churches hold investment portfolios. If not, in any case local churches belong to annual conferences, synods, presbyteries, dioceses, etc., which bodies ordinarily have endowment funds used for investment purposes.

Sometimes these portfolios are carefully screened to see that they include companies producing life-supportive goods and services, and sometimes they are not. Sometimes investments are reviewed to note their connection with weapons production, and sometimes not.

Local churches have an opportunity to strengthen their peace witness through seeing that their own investment portfolios or those of their judicatory (larger church connectional body) are respectfully "clean." Jesus once said: "Where your treasure is, there will your heart be also." (Matt. 6:21) If the church has invested in makers of bombs, then that reflects its values in reality.

So if your church doesn't have any investments, ask your larger church body for a detailed list of their investments. Then review them to see that all are in the life-supportive category, such as housing, food, health care, pollution control, appliances, clothing, education, and leisure time. These could well include such positive securities as the Federal National Mortgage Association (low interest loans for mortgages) and World Bank bonds. A large proportion of the profits of the World Bank goes to the International Development Association for long term, low interest loans to the poorer nations of the world.

You can secure a list of the "One Hundred Largest Defense Contractors" from the Department of Defense and may not want to be invested in these companies. Not to be invested in weapons-related firms means not only staying out of companies producing bombs and ammunition but also avoiding firms representing international oil, electronics, space and aviation, automobiles, and computers (World War III is ready to go with the press of a computer button). Even avoidance of such stocks leaves a large pool of attractive companies with yield and growth potential.

Remember, as you make your review, no company is perfect; the choice reverts to one of better and worse. But this is where the real world choices are always made. And do not be deceived by the names of companies in relation to their holdings. Honeywell manufactures the guidance systems for nuclear missiles; Coca Cola owns a distillery.

If you would like some help from a model project which has made these sophisticated distinctions since 1971, write to Pax World Fund for a prospectus and auxiliary information. Their address is 224 State Street, Portsmouth, New Hampshire 03801. The author was one of the initiators of Pax.

Human Rights Day. Many church people, because they are ardent believers in freedom, would like to do something in the field of human rights. One simple way to do this would be to observe Human Rights Day on December 10. This is the day that the Universal Declaration of Human Rights was signed in 1948.

Such an ambitious project could be sponsored by the churches of a local community or of the resident county. This could be done in cooperation with the United Nations Association. One of the better models for such an observance has been the Human Rights Day luncheon held each year in Washington, D. C. This event is sponsored by the metropolitan area U.N.A., and church representatives cooperate fully.

At this luncheon, U.N.A. members and other interested parties attend. Representatives of the diplomatic corps are invited as guests. In your situation you can invite consular officials from a nearby city or at least a delegation of foreign students.

The speaker at this Human Rights Day affair is always a specialist in that field. He or she could be from the government, the United Nations, the university, or from a human rights group like Amnesty International.

At one point in the program all attendees are asked to read together the Preamble to the Universal Declaration of Human Rights, which upholds the Declaration as "a common standard of achievement for all peoples and all nations. . . ."

One of the outstanding features of the Washington, D. C. observance is the honoring of persons in the community who have promoted human rights. In the case of the capital city, this may rise to several dozen persons every year, with each one nominated by a community group. In most communities, such an award could go to just one person each year.

In this way the observance is able to recognize the truth of a memorable observation once made by Eleanor Roosevelt, who served as U.S. Special Representative on Human Rights:

> Where, after all, do universal human rights begin? In small places, close to home—so close and so small that they cannot be seen on any map of the world. Yet they are the world of the individual person; the neighborhood he lives in; the school or college he attends; the factory, farm or office where he works. Such are the places where every man, woman and child seeks equal justice, equal opportunity, equal dignity without discrimination. Unless these rights have meaning there, they have little meaning anywhere. . . .[16]

Groups wishing to support the Genocide Convention as a human rights issue may want to prepare themselves for the struggle. The Convention is expected to come before the Senate for ratification in 1981, according to Senator William Proxmire, who has been its leading proponent.

World Hunger. There are many projects around the country which relate to the world hunger issue. But one of the more imaginative programs was one initiated by the Grace United Methodist Church of Minneapolis. They have established a cooperative food-buying project called Care & Share, through which the savings are channeled to various world hunger and human needs concerns.

Care & Share operates on a biweekly schedule. Every other Sunday mimeographed order blanks listing the items to be purchased are available at the church. Normally the list is limited to fresh fruits and vegetables, cheese, and eggs. But at six-week intervals it is possible to place orders for nonperishables, such as rice, flour, dried milk, peanut butter, and honey.

Purchases are then made from a wholesaler and individual orders are prepared for pickup on Friday evening or Saturday morning. Volunteers make deliveries to shut-ins and those without transportation. At delivery time the bill shows the difference between the actual cost and the comparable cost at retail, usually about 30 to 40%. Most parishioners are able then to contribute the savings to the Care & Share Fund. But there is no pressure and it is considered quite all right if a family needs the savings to help out with its own budget.

As a result of the accumulated savings, the church has been able to contribute thousands of dollars to such causes as United Methodist Committee on Relief, the victims of the Guatemalan earthquake, and the sponsorship of Vietnam refugees.

Surely a useful project like this is adaptable to most any church, large or small, in the nation. It does take a lot of dedicated volunteers willing to perform a very helpful service. But isn't this what the church is all about?

Peace Comes in Pieces. Peace comes in pieces. It doesn't drop out of the sky all at once, nor is it achieved through one bold stroke in the direction of international goodwill. It comes through patient plodding and persistent probing. The question is: will the church be one of those pieces, a part of the whole that leads to world harmony?

Were the church suddenly to decide to devote as much effort and money to the cause of peace as the state extracts from its people for the prosecution of war, then the unfinished dome of the U.N. General Assembly might be crowned with a wreath of olive branches.

But what if, despite the endeavors of Christians and other responsible citizens, the struggle for peace fails? Should nuclear war come, and firestorms rage, and cities topple, archaeologists of a future generation, in digging through silt layers of once radioactive dust, may come upon a copper box. This receptacle, laid in the cornerstone of the Church Center for the United Nations in 1962 will, when opened, be found to contain such items as a copy of the National Council of Churches emphasis on peace, the pamphlet "A Christian Primer of the United Nations," a Peace Convenanter's Card, and a folder describing a "Race for Peace" program.[17] The New Breed, much wiser than the old irrational and inflexible generation, will nod to one another and say: "The church tried. . . ."

PART TWO

VARIOUS MODELS FOR THE PROPHETIC COMMUNITY

The prophetic community emerges and becomes visible as soon as a need is identified and a decision is made to do something about it. It may begin in response to an emergency cry for food, clothing, or shelter and gain strength in solving longer-range needs and eliminating root causes of basic probems. Or it may simply evolve out of a commitment to feed the hungry, care for the sick and lonely, and help those who cannot help themselves.

A two-year search for "prophetic communities" across the nation led us to: (1) churches and congregations of many denominations and faiths; (2) councils and associations that bring together many religious groups, and often secular organizations and government agencies, into a working relationship to attain common goals; and (3) individuals who share a vision for witnessing, education, service, and action in a specific area in the name of God. The great majority of our responses were from Christian churches and councils, though this does not mean that other faiths may not be as prophetic. Since we were writing from a Christian perspective, our search tended to lead us to the Christian community.

The directory that follows includes descriptions of more than 100 projects chosen because they are worthy of serving as models for others to adopt or adapt. Some programs are purely social education, while others are social service or social action—or both. Some are all three.

Literally thousands of churches now have emergency food banks, clothes closets or thrift shops, meals on wheels for the homebound, and day-care programs for children. In many instances, several churches and agencies have combined efforts to work more effectively. Only samplings of these projects are included in the directory.

Many of the programs listed are familiar to us. We have either visited the projects or had the opportunity to speak with persons involved. However, information for many other projects is lifted from data provided on survey sheets and in printed brochures. Particulars may change from year to year, yet the general concept of the projects will still be useful as a model for others with similar concerns.

The name of each program is followed with limited descriptive material. For additional information, contact the church or agency given at the bottom of the section. Where the name of a director or pastor is known, it is given. The price in parentheses is a requested amount for a reply and is subject to change. In all other cases, we suggest a contribution of 50 cents to a dollar with a self-addressed, stamped envelope.

May this directory help your church, group, or agency on the road to becoming a prophetic community.

Readers are encouraged to send information on social education, social service, and social action programs not mentioned in this book and to update the projects listed. This material will be considered in revisions of *Becoming a Prophetic Community*.

Please send information to: Elizabeth S. Smith
2946 M Street, S. E.
Washington, D. C. 20019

Model Categories

Adult and Senior Citizen Programs **102**
Advocacy Programs **116**
Children's Programs **124**
Criminal Justice/Prison Ministries **130**
Disaster Relief Programs **135**
Education/Information Programs **139**
Health and Counseling Programs **146**
Housing Programs **154**
Hunger Programs **162**
Multiservice Programs **168**
Peace Programs **178**
Rural Programs **182**
Youth Programs **190**

Adult and Senior Citizen Programs

1. Emmaus Services for the Aging
2. The Shepherd's Center (Kansas City, Missouri)
3. CHUM Church
4. Retired Senior Volunteer Program (RSVP)
5. The Shepherd's Center (New Orleans, Louisiana)
6. Family Resource Center
7. The Handyperson Maintenance Service
8. Lakeside Elder Adult Project
9. The Closet, Inc.
10. Friendship Center
11. Full Employment Project
12. Job Information/Resource Bank
13. The Parent-Child Center
14. Adult Day Care Center

§

Emmaus Services for the Aging

Five congregations in the inner city of Washington, D.C. share in a community ministry under the name of Emmaus Fellowship. One of the newer projects, Emmaus Services for the Aging, was initiated in 1978 to identify older people and their needs in the geographic community in which the churches are located.

Volunteers spent nine months in a survey of one hundred people. Even as results were being analyzed, follow-up services were beginning where special needs had been found. A year later, church workers involved in the program see three distinct stages of outreach.

The first stage is meeting people. This hasn't always been easy. As Emmaus volunteers have focused on getting into locked apartment buildings, they have needed invitations to enter. They have met people in four main ways:

—by asking older members of the five Emmaus churches if they would be interviewed and give names of friends;

—by visiting lunch clubs in the neighborhood and interviewing persons then and there;

—by asking resident managers for help;

—by talking to people sitting on their stoops, by carrying groceries, and sometimes through neighborhood activities.

The most successful volunteers have been community residents, and recently one of these was hired to help Emmaus increase its contacts. He has added MacDonald's, the local druggist, and his own acquaintances as sources for leads.

The second stage of outreach is the response to requests for information and aid. Very often, volunteers discover that an inquiry about homemaking services masks a deeper need for companionship and help with shopping. Or a person asking about food stamps may really be saying that the rent is too high. The rent may use up most of the monthly income, leaving little for the other necessities of life. When one person sought information on food stamps and Medicare, volunteers discovered that the gas and electricity had been turned off for a year!

In the second stage, all expressed needs are taken at face value. However, volunteers have come to accept that a request of any kind for aid is a sign that other needs exist, so they keep the conversation and visits going in any way they can. Later, they may find such underlying problems as loneliness, depression, alcoholism, and illiteracy.

The third stage of outreach comes when people begin to share needs of the heart—concerns for a grandchild or other family members, the wish to set their affairs in order.

Workers with the Emmaus Services for the Aging agree that the word "outreach" acquires new and greater dimensions as it commits them to listen, to respond, and to care.

The churches that make up the Emmaus Fellowship are Foundry United Methodist Church, First Baptist Church of the City of Washington, Metropolitan A.M.E. Church, Luther Place Memorial Church, and the National City Christian Church.

Emmaus Services for the Aging, National City Christian Church, Thomas Circle, Washington, D.C. 20005. Diane Amussen, Director.

§

The Shepherd's Center (Kansas City, Missouri)

This program, designed to provide senior citizens with meaningful experiences and an alternative to institutional care, has already become the model for numerous other groups working with the elderly. Because of it, Central United Methodist Church in Kansas City, Missouri received *Guideposts'* Church Award in 1978.

Some years ago, Dr. Elbert C. Cole, pastor of Central Church, called a group of ministers and laypersons together to consider building a retirement home. However, the Chicago firm requested to do the feasibility study reported that only 5% of those over 65 live in retirement and nursing homes. This raised the question of how the needs of the other 95% might be met. The answers began to come when it was observed that five retired men were finding real joy in delivering meals on wheels, hot meals for the homebound, at noon each day.

The Shepherd's Center came into being in the summer of 1972 under the sponsorship of 22 churches and synagogues and with a $25,000 federal Older Americans Act grant. Services that first year included meals on wheels, volunteers shopping for or with elderly citizens, clergy on call 24 hours a day for a crisis situation, and an Adventures in Learning program that offered 15 different subjects in a nine-week course. There were 215 volunteers involved and over 1,500 senior citizens were served by the Center's programs.

In 1978, 25 churches and synagogues were supporting and participating in the operation of the Center, which is incorporated with a board of directors of 24 community residents. The Shepherd's Center no longer depends upon federal funding; the budget is completely underwritten by the contributions of sponsoring churches, organizations, foundations, community groups, and individuals.

Additional home services being offered were:

—Wheels That Care, transportation to medical facilities with volunteer drivers;

—Handyman, small repairs—electrical, minor plumbing, carpentry, and even some painting—made by retired, skilled workers for a small fee;

—Friendly Visitors, home visits and telephone calls made to many homebound persons by individuals through community organizations;

—Companion Aides, light housekeeping, meal preparation, and other chores performed for a small fee;

—Care XX, free meals and homemaker services as needed by persons with limited incomes;
—Security and Protection, information on home security and personal protection offered by crime-prevention aides.

A Life Enrichment Center brings together older people who need help, love, and understanding as they move through the loss of a loved one or other traumatic experiences. At the same time it provides support, participants are being helped to find new life and new hope.

The Health Enrichment Center offers a number of services and classes in an effort to help senior citizens maintain their health. Personal health continues to be the major concern of most older people.

On Tuesdays, the Center attracts many to its Creative Workshops, with one of the most popular being on clock repairing. There were also workshops in 1978 on various arts and crafts, genealogy, folk dancing, and conversational French and Spanish. Lunch is served by reservation for a nominal price.

Fridays bring hundreds to attend the Adventures in Learning nine-week courses. Registration is only $4.00 and participants can attend as many of the 37 classes offered as time will permit. Travelogues, speed reading, international affairs, various languages, bridge, book reviews, needlework, exercise classes, and chess are but a few of the listings. A hot lunch is served for $1.00.

Even a National Defensive Driving Course was offered for a very low fee with privileges to attend both the Creative Workshops and Adventures in Learning courses.

The Shepherd's Center, with Dr. Cole continuing as executive director, is putting meaning into the lives of thousands of senior citizens in the Country Club-Waldo area of Kansas City because they give as well as receive. Most of the Center's programs depend upon volunteers and the majority of these are coming from the age group being served. The Center has grown because it is a community venture that is willing to change with the needs.

The Shepherd's Center, 5218 Oak Street, Kansas City, Missouri 64112. Dr. Elbert C. Cole, Executive Director; Joseph Scanlon, Director.

§

CHUM Church

The Central Hillside United Ministry (CHUM), an ecumenical grouping in central Duluth, Minnesota, moved forward in 1974 with a dream to serve the social, emotional, and spiritual needs of retarded adults in the community. CHUM Church would offer skills, faith enrichment, and fellowship for developmentally disabled individuals with the hope that within three years they would be able to function in a church setting of their own choosing. In the meantime, CHUM member churches (11 in 1978) would be prepared to accept and integrate the CHUM Church "graduates" into their fellowships.

In 1977 the original goals were reaffirmed, but it was recognized that the integration of some participants into other congregations would be impossible. In looking back over the first three years, it was agreed that CHUM Church had succeeded in giving retarded people a better understanding of their relationship with God. There had been increasing involvement of members in worship experiences with an increasing awareness of what a worship service is all about. Fellowship activities had encouraged feelings of self-worth. Perhaps the greatest gains came on the other side. Clergy and laypersons assisting in the CHUM Church programs were becoming sensitized and educated to the needs of the developmentally disabled and were overcoming their stereotyping of the retarded.

CHUM Church services are held once a month. Coordination of the needed volunteers has been simplified through the development of the Helper Church program. Each month, one church arranges for the minister, the special music, assistants for both classes and the worship service, hosts for the social hour, and drivers for the two buses and four cars needed to transport the approximately 75 who come regularly.

Goals, priorities, and policies are determined by a Program Board of 18, representing many groups and agencies of the community. Members include CHUM Church participants, parents of participants, social workers, group home leaders, educators, and agency people involved with mentally retarded people. A full-time coordinator is employed to oversee the CHUM Church program, assist with fund proposals, and present the CHUM Church story to interested groups and through the media.

Future goals call for the developing of new religious education materials, resources for worship, and a song book. Teacher training programs are to be upgraded and an ongoing pool of volunteer teachers maintained. New ways will be sought for better utilization of the volunteers from Helper Churches.

CHUM Church will continue to welcome and serve the developmentally disabled of Duluth.

Central Hillside United Ministry. Dan Moore, CHUM Church Coordinator, First United Methodist Church, 230 East Skyline Parkway, Duluth, Minnesota 55811.

§

Retired Senior Volunteer Program (RSVP)

Over 250,000 citizens who are 60 years of age and over are now volunteering their services through nearly 700 RSVP programs in 50 states, Puerto Rico, the Virgin Islands, Guam, and the District of Columbia. These volunteers serve on a regular but part-time basis in a variety of settings throughout their communities. RSVP functions under the auspices of an established community service organization with some funding, support, and technical assistance from ACTION, the federal volunteer agency.

Six percent or more of the RSVP programs are sponsored by church groups, such as the Interfaith Community Services of St. Joseph, Missouri. Drawing on the large number of senior citizens in both Buchanan and Andrew Counties, the RSVP program of I.C.S. has more than 600 volunteers giving 45,000 hours of service each year to community organizations.

The opportunities for service are unlimited. In St. Joseph, the RSVP volunteers are piecing quilts for distribution to low-income families, serving meals at three nutrition sites, taking meals to homebound residents, visiting and serving in nursing homes and hospitals, and helping in day-care and Head Start programs. Their square dance group and choir entertain regularly in nursing homes and other institutions.

For information on *RSVP of Buchanan and Andrew Counties,* write to Interfaith Community Services, 200 Cherokee Street, St. Joseph, Missouri 64505. Gwendolyn Marlin, RSVP Supervisor.

For general information on RSVP, contact your regional ACTION office. Or you can write to your state Office on Aging, or to RSVP, ACTION, Washington, D. C. 20525.

§

The Shepherd's Center (New Orleans, Louisiana)

This particular center is an ecumenical ministry of nine Protestant and Catholic churches incorportated under the name of Lakeview Area Senior Ministry in New Orleans, Louisiana.

The purpose of the Shepherd's Center is to identify and respond to the needs of the elderly residents in the Lakeview-Lake Vista area. It seeks to alleviate the social and physical isolation of older persons by providing services which will minister to the spiritual and emotional needs of the whole person.

The Shepherd's Center ministry is organized into three divisions: the Drop-in Center, the Adventures-in-Learning program, and direct services. Any older person in the metropolitan area of New Orleans is invited to participate in the activities at the Drop-in Center and to enroll for the Adventures-in-Learning classes. To be eligible for emergency services, a recipient must live in a designated zip code area.

Though similar to the Shepherd's Center in Kansas City, Missouri, the experiences of the New Orleans staff and volunteers might provide some new insights for those considering programs for the elderly. In this Center, the staff members are a Director/Coordinator, a Visitor/Case Finder, and a Secretary/Bookkeeper. The three divisions of work are headed by volunteers, and many volunteers are involved in teaching and directing the various activities. The final administrative responsibility lies with the Board of Directors, elected by supporting churches.

The Shepherd's Center, 5931 Milne, New Orleans, Louisiana 70124. Lillian Reynolds, Director/Coordinator. (50¢)

§

Family Resource Center

The Family Resource Center is a project of N.E.W.S. (Neighborhood Ecumenical Witness and Service), sponsored jointly by the Grace United Presbyterian Church and the Independence Avenue United Methodist Church of Kansas City, Missouri.

N.E.W.S. is convinced that parents are still the world's greatest experts in determining the needs of their children. Since much of the child-rearing is assumed by institutions of society in which parents have little power, parents are often left feeling frustrated, guilty, and inadequate when their children fail to function well or to achieve at an expected level. N.E.W.S. believes that professional services usually increase the power of the professionals and diminish the capabilities of the family.

The Family Resource Center seeks to bring parents and families together in small neighborhood groups to share skills and knowledge and to select their own experts for assistance with family problems. Each group will be a self-help collective that is racially and economically integrated. Priorities will be limited by need and geography. Services will be centralized, and parents will be encouraged to participate in choosing paraprofessionals and volunteers living in the community to assist them. Stress will be placed on programs that will help families remain together.

Family Resource Center, N.E.W.S., 811 Benton Boulevard, Kansas City, Missouri 64124. Contact either Marcia E. Johnson or Ronald T. Roberts.

§

The Handyperson Maintenance Service

Inter/Serv (Interfaith Community Services) in St. Joseph, Missouri has an extensive program for senior citizens that includes everything from housing, educational opportunities, and general services to such leisure time activities as dance contests with prizes and trips to Kansas City for shopping and ball games.

The Handyperson Home Maintenance Service available to persons 60 years of age and older particularly attracted our attention. (See page 53.) This is a two-way program designed to benefit both the elderly homeowner or apartment dweller with maintenance or repair problems and the retired person who needs to augment his or her income or who simply wants to help others.

The main purpose of the service is to help senior citizens to remain in their homes by providing assistance with the upkeep of their properties. Clients pay for materials used on the job and contribute, if able, toward the labor cost of the services provided.

Started as a six-month program to run from April through September 1978, federal funds for the project came from the Northwest Missouri Area Agency on Aging, Title III funding by the Department of Social Services, Missouri Office of Aging under the provisions of the Older Americans Act of 1965, as amended.

Bee Hive Senior Citizen Center, c/o Interfaith Community Services, 200 Cherokee Street, St. Joseph, Missouri 64505. Beverly Graham and Judith Harper, Supervisors.

§

Lakeside Elder Adult Project

The Crescent Avenue Church in Fort Wayne, Indiana came to the realization in 1974 that 85% of its members had moved from the area in which the church was located. However, the church was continuing to reach out to neighborhood residents, most of them elderly, through a community garden, a food co-op, and a luncheon program prepared and served by church volunteers. A commitment was made to see what else could be done to meet the needs of older people, and so the Lakeside Elder Adult Project began to evolve.

A visit to the Shepherd's Center in Kansas City convinced Crescent Avenue members that a similar program could be as effective in Fort Wayne. They began with Learning Adventures, a series of courses on a wide variety of subjects. The response was overwhelming. The creative writing class even published the better works in a book that promptly sold out the first printing. Soon senior citizens were coming from all over the city to learn and grow.

Craft Adventures became the second step in the Crescent Avenue Church project. Courses on knitting, weaving, and quilting proved so popular that other crafts were offered until 22 courses were running concurrently. In both Learning Adventures and Craft Adventures, all teachers were volunteers and space was donated by the church.

With so many beautiful craft items being created, the next logical step seemed to be the opening of a shop in which these articles could be sold. Handcraft shops in Ohio, New York, and North Carolina were visited, as well as ones closer to home. After three months of planning, talking, and writing, a first-year grant was received through the Older Americans Act to cover 90% of the cash needed for programming.

The space problem was not solved quite so easily. The search committee failed to find a suitable site for the amount budgeted for rent. However, before giving up the whole idea, the church sponsored a three-day craft fair to test the response. Items were displayed by 130 older people and more than $5,000 was realized in sales.

About this same time, a house next to the church was placed on the market. Funding for the craft shop could not be used for purchasing property—only for rental. After much discussion and planning, the church trustees agreed to buy the house and one individual lent the amount of the down payment. Others succeeded in raising the $13,000 necessary to replace the heating system, build a garage, convert rooms into craft and wordworking shops, etc. More than 300 people supplied thousands of hours of work until all shelves and cabinets were in place and the papering and painting were done.

Elder Artisans is now open six days a week and is staffed almost entirely by retired volunteers. It has become a gathering place for those wishing to use the craft and woodworking shops and by those wanting to make purchases.

Out of this has grown a new program, the Saturday Sampler. In this, senior citizens are conducting a series of all-day workshops for interested persons of all ages. Thus those who could not qualify for Craft Adventures because they were not yet 60 can now learn new crafts.

The Lakeside Elder Adult Project continues to expand. A transportation service for the elderly has been started that uses drivers of all ages, and Elder Helpers will make simple home repairs. Another popular program is Travel Adventures, which plans and conducts trips of one-to-ten days in length for about half the cost of professional tours.

Members of the Lakeside Elder Adult Project have discovered that they can move mountains. They see the opportunities for future programs and service as limitless.

Lakeside Elder Adult Project, The Crescent Avenue United Methodist Church, 1232 Crescent Avenue, Fort Wayne, Indiana 46805. The Reverend Charles Ellinwood, Pastor.

§

The Closet, Inc.

Many churches and organizations across the country maintain clothes cupboards or thrift shops to provide good, clean, used clothing and small household articles at nominal prices.

One such program is the Closet, sponsored by churches and civic groups of the Herndon, Reston, and Sterling areas in northern Virginia. Now self-supporting, the Closet has a paid manager and occupies rented quarters. However, all articles are donated and volunteers from the participating churches serve as staff. The Closet is open three days a week from 10:00 A.M. until 2:00 P.M.

Periodically, items that have not sold are boxed and sent to Appalachia. All monies accumulated above expenses are given to worthy projects that directly or indirectly benefit low-income families in the community.

The Closet is run by a management council composed of two representatives from each participating church and organization. The council meets quarterly with the executive committee meeting according to need.

One of the goals of the Closet is to encourage community involvement, and the success of the project would indicate this goal is being met.

The Closet, Inc., c/o Mrs. Lola C. Washington, 11222 South Shore Road, Reston, Virginia 22090. (50¢)

Friendship Center

Center City Churches, Inc., an organization of eight downtown churches in Hartford, Connecticut, opened the Friendship Center in July 1971, primarily to serve the alcoholic and lonely adults of the city. Friendship Center, open every day of the year, is dedicated to providing a drop-in center that offers a place to visit, rest, and eat, and where each person entering is accepted and given the help and support he or she needs.

Since its beginning, the Center has had to move to larger quarters and both program and staff have been enlarged. Today the Center offers food services, clothing, counseling, small groups, and employment opportunities. Many visitors with problems are guided to agencies that are a part of a vast network of referral services.

From 7:00 A.M. until 4:00 P.M. each day, about 140 visitors are welcomed to the Center. Food is served three times: coffee and pastry in the morning, sandwiches at eleven, and hot food at three in the afternoon. Holiday dinners are festive celebrations served in the VFW Hall in Hartford to 200. Periodic picnics in the country are popular and offer a day of relaxation and sports away from the city.

A monthly newsletter is prepared and distributed to nearly 1,000 persons concerned with alcoholism and related problems. In this way the needs of the men and women of the Center are shared widely.

Center City Churches, Inc., 170 Main Street, Hartford, Connecticut 06106. Rafael Gonzalez, Director of Friendship Center.

§

Full Employment Project

The Des Moines Area Urban Mission Council of the United Methodist Church sought to alleviate unemployment by organizing the unemployed and soliciting community support.

The first step was the hiring of an Organizer/Job Developer from among the unemployed to aid other unemployed persons in their search for employment, to develop job opportunities, and to assist in the establishing of training and support programs. Within the first year he organized Jobless United, a group of unemployed willing to work together to eliminate common barriers to their finding suitable employment while providing support for each other.

At the same time, concerned persons from the religious community, employment organizations, and other civic groups were formed into a support group called the Full Employment Coalition. Coalition members have helped formulate guidelines for the Organizer, sought funding, monitored the program of the state Job Service, encouraged state and national labor legislation, and increased community awareness of the problems of the unemployed. (See page 57 of the text for further details.)

Full Employment Project, Des Moines Area Urban Mission Council, 921 Pleasant Street, Des Moines, Iowa 50309. The Reverend Ken Fineran, Urban Minister. (25¢)

§

Job Information/Resource Bank

This is a ministry of the Metropolitan Learning Center of the Los Angeles Council of Churches, designed to train participants between the ages of 18 and 50 in developing a community Job Information/Resource Bank.

With unemployment running as high as 15% in some of the areas surveyed, there was an obvious need to provide employment information, counseling, and training programs for unskilled, semi-skilled and unemployed persons. Many were young or among the hard-core unemployed, such as veterans and ex-offenders. Counseling and training include such topics as job-seeking methods, interview dynamics, quality work performance, on-the-job conflict, and career options. Field offices are now open in six communities, most in local churches.

The Job Information/Resource Bank also provides information to minority businesses on training and technical assistance opportunities. The employment capacity of these businesses increases as financial stability is attained.

The primary goal of the overall program is to improve the quality of community life by raising local socio-economic levels.

Job Information/Resource Bank, Los Angeles Council of Churches, 760 South Westmoreland Avenue, Suite 364-70, Los Angeles, California 90005. Ms. Mildred L. Arnold, Executive Director. ($1.00)

The Parent-Child Center

The Inter-Church Council Pastoral Care & Counseling Services, Inc. of New Bedford, Massachusetts set four goals for its Parent-Child Center, which serves an area that includes nine towns. They are:

—to make the homes of abused/neglected children safer and more satisfying environments for children and parents by offering supportive services to parents;

—to provide supportive outreach services to parents with difficulties who are not receiving services elsewhere;

—to increase community awareness around the issue of child abuse/neglect and what everyone can do to help;

—to strive to coordinate community efforts to provide the most direct and helpful services to abused/neglected families.

To carry out these objectives, the Center provides a variety of services to individuals, families, and the community.

Lay therapists, all parents themselves, visit parents in their homes on a "friend-to-friend" basis. They provide long-term supportive relationships, helping parents meet emotional and material needs. Therapists are on call on a 24-hour basis for any emergency or crisis.

Support groups have been formed for parents who feel alone and pressured by the responsibilities and difficulties of parenting. Led by male-female cotherapists who help set up an atmosphere of trust and sharing, group participants can share with each other common problems, concerns, and frustrations.

A Parents Anonymous group is sponsored by the Center for parents who wish to overcome the abuse and neglect of their children. This is a self-help organization.

The Center also provides ten-week Family Effectiveness Training courses that are open to the public. Emphasis is placed on the developing and improving of communication skills within the family. Those who can are asked for a donation to cover expenses, but no interested person is turned away.

Any person with questions about child abuse or neglect can call the Parent-Child Center for confidential information and referral. A resource library containing books, films, and pamphlets is open to parents, students, community groups, and professionals. Many of these materials may be borrowed.

The Parent-Child Center also has speakers willing to meet with community, church, and school groups on issues relating to child development and child abuse/neglect. Community workshops are conducted at intervals throughout the year.

The Parent-Child Center, Inter-Church Council Pastoral Care & Counseling Center, 412 County Street, New Bedford, Massachusetts 02740. Contact person: Tom Amisson, M.S.W. (50¢)

§

Adult Day Care Center

An increasing number of adult day-care centers are being established over the country to provide protective, rehabilitative, and restorative services for the elderly who are having difficulty maintaining their independence and remaining in their own homes, but who do not require institutional care. In many cases families are relieved of some of the responsibility for the care of their loved ones.

Such a program for the senior citizens of Orange County, Florida is sponsored by the Citizens' Advisory Council on Aging, Inc. with the assistance of community services and organizations. The Concord Park United Methodist Church has provided rent-free space and volunteers to work with the program.

The Adult Day Care Center in Orlando is open daily Monday through Friday between the hours of 8:00 A.M. and 5:00 P.M. Most of those participating in the program are frail, moderately handicapped, or slightly confused.

The Center seeks to provide an overall therapeutic environment composed of a variety of services and activities to meet basic and special needs of the elderly. These include limited transportation, a noon meal and snacks, nutrition and health education, counseling and referral, exercise and recreation, arts and crafts, special programs and activities. A licensed nurse is always on duty.

Eligibility is based on the demonstrated need for the service.

Adult Day Care Center, Orange County Citizens' Advisory Council on Aging, Inc., 113 East Central Boulevard, Orlando, Florida 32801.

Advocacy Programs

1. Religious Influence on Leaders
2. New Mexico Coalition Against Hunger
3. Fair Share Housing Center
4. Action of Church and Community Together (ACCT)
5. Metro Ministry
6. The Delta Ministry
7. The Hunger Network in Ohio, Michigan, and Kentucky
8. Energy Conservation Campaign
9. Green Community Services

§

Religious Influence on Leaders

This interfaith coalition of Protestant, Catholic, and Jewish leaders in Wisconsin began with a group of concerned United Methodists in 1973. They wanted to make their personal opinions on such issues as peace and poverty known to national leaders responsible for making decisions. There had to be communication if influence was to be exerted.

Even as leaders were meeting to decide on specific issues of interest—such as poverty, armament spending, integrity in government, energy alternatives, and amnesty—efforts were proceeding to organize within each of the nine congressional districts of the state. Through the years, district groups have met with their congresspersons to voice concerns and recommendations. Delegations also meet with Wisconsin's U.S. senators.

Groups are always careful to explain that they speak only for themselves. However, such meetings do provide the opportunity to present official policy positions taken by church bodies on concrete issues.

Religious Influence on Leaders. Dr. Ray E. Short, Professor of Sociology, University of Wisconsin, Madison, Wisconsin 53706.

Impact, 110 Maryland Avenue, N. E., Washington, D. C. 20002, is a national legislative network operated by the religious community that will be glad to provide information for the organizing and implementing of a "grass-roots" effort similar to that above.

New Mexico Coalition Against Hunger

This coalition of persons and groups working to eliminate hunger has gradually developed a five-fold program of advocacy. Though the first four efforts are listed, special attention is called to the newest project—Public Service Announcements on the Food Stamp Program.

The New Mexico Coalition Against Hunger has a *Legislative Advocacy* program that moves from identifying major hunger issues at national, state, and local levels to doing something about them. This involves working with other advocacy groups to research and study the effect of specific issues and programs in New Mexico, direct and phone/mail lobbying, establishing a network among constituents to coordinate efforts, and monitoring the operation of federal food and nutrition programs in the state.

The New Mexico Coalition promotes *Self-Help Development* by encouraging food co-ops and buying clubs, producer-consumer cooperatives, community gardens, food banks (food salvage networks), land banking, and land trusts.

A *Food Stamp Project* monitors the Food Stamp Program in the Albuquerque area.

The Coalition is concerned with *Farmworker Issues* and demonstrates this interest by working with farmworker-based organizations with an emphasis on issues relating to food and nutrition. Consideration is also being given to initiating an effort in New Mexico for comprehensive farmworker legislation.

The fifth aspect of the Coalition's program deals with the *Media*. It has moved from just promoting the Coalition's activities and the publishing of a newsletter to developing, distributing and airing Public Service Announcements on television and radio. Each P.S.A. is 30 or 60 seconds long and provides food stamp information. Local personalities and actors have participated in the preparation of these dramatic-style spots. There is limited transitional and summary narrative, and the last few seconds of each P.S.A. is reserved for the insertion of local information. The spots are available in Spanish as well as English.

Conceived at the time of a change in the Food Stamp Program, the Public Service Announcements were designed so each would cover one specific piece of information. The first describes food stamps and why qualified persons should participate in the program. Others deal with the rights of the applicants, the responsibilities of the Food Stamp Office, and the elimination of the purchase requirement. Funding has come through grants and contributions, including support of church denominations.

New Mexico Coalition Against Hunger, P. O. Box 80022, Albuquerque, New Mexico 87198. Eduardo Díaz, State Coordinator. (25¢)

Fair Share Housing Center

In 1975 the New Jersey Supreme Court ordered the suburbs to "open their doors" to the urban and rural poor and to permit the suburban development of subsidized housing for low- and moderate-income families. Each "developing" suburban municipality was directed to provide the opportunity for the development of its "fair share" of the regional need of housing for the poor. Directly involved, then and now, are the township of Mount Laurel and the city of Camden.

The township of Mount Laurel is a growing community representative of suburbia, though within its boundaries is an area housing descendants of the first residents—mostly poor and black. The city of Camden has seen an exodus of white families, leaving a current population of approximately 15,000 elderly who cannot escape and 65,000 minorities excluded from the suburbs. Implementation of the 1975 *Mount Laurel* decision will ease the fiscal pressures of the city by requiring the suburbs to share in the responsibility for providing housing for the less fortunate.

The Fair Share Housing Center is a nonprofit citizens' group working to implement the Mount Laurel case through community education and the development of "fair share" housing models. An 18-month demonstration program calls for three steps in working with the residents of Cherry Hill, Moorestown, and Mount Laurel:

— "Community Profiles" will be published and distributed to the residents in each community. These profiles will show the community as it is and as it could become with future development.

— "Site selection" reports will be prepared to give each municipality an idea of how it could include low- and moderate-income housing to fulfill its "fair share" responsibility without having an adverse impact on the community.

— Proposed time schedules for the development of "fair share" housing in each of the three communities will be distributed and discussed with residents.

This demonstration project of the Fair Share Housing Center is being supported by the Camden Metropolitan Ministry, West Jersey Presbytery, and Synod of the Northeast (Presbyterians), the American Baptist Churches of New Jersey (Baptists), the New Jersey Synod (Lutherans), and the multi-denominational Moorestown Community of Churches. Other churches and groups are also involved. Funding is dependent solely on individual contributions, church support, and foundation grants.

The program brings together architects, attorneys, business persons, engineers, planners, clergy, psychologists, sociologists, and community residents interested in the "fair share" housing concept.

Fair Share Housing Center, Inc., 510 Park Boulevard, Cherry Hill, New Jersey 08034. Contact: Kathy Claxton.

§

Action of Church and Community Together (ACCT)

The ACCT Council is the community service and social action arm of The Downtown United Presbyterian Church of Rochester, New York. It supports and is involved in programs of criminal justice, community organization, housing, and survival against poverty. ACCT also sponsors a Sunday morning adult education and discussion class for the study of current and critical social issues. Most subjects are pursued over a period of several weeks with leaders chosen for their expertise in a given field.

Following a church-wide emphasis on world hunger led by ACCT in 1977, a Lifestyle Covenant Group was formed to explore lifestyle changes that would respond to the eco-justice/world hunger crisis.

The ACCT Council has continually tried to find new ways to relate the resources of the church to the fight against the deterioration and abandonment of downtown and urban neighborhood property. This resulted in ACCT recommending to the session of The Downtown United Presbyterian Church that:

- —lending institutions be advised that the church deplored any type of discrimination in granting mortgages.
- —church funds be deposited in institutions having favorable city mortgage lending policies.
- —a bank be encouraged, as an act of good faith in promoting home ownership in the city, to publicly declare this intent.

Following this action, the church trustees transferred $40,000 to a bank with an investment policy more favorable to the city. A statement of church policy accompanied the letter opening the new account.

ACCT encourages the use of church facilities for forums, conferences, and workshops on social issues and for open meetings of community groups. Office space has been granted to such groups as the Women's Prison Project, Project VIE (Volunteers Intervening for Equity), and Parents Anonymous.

Goals of the ACCT Council are under constant study and revision to reflect current needs in the church and community.

The ACCT Council, The Downtown United Presbyterian Church, 121 North Fitzhugh Street, Rochester, New York 14614.

Metro Ministry

Metro Ministry, which began as a mission outreach program of the Springfield District, West Ohio Conference of the United Methodist Church a decade ago, is moving more and more into an advocacy role. It sees societal problems calling for institutional changes that will bring reconciliation between people, classes, and communities with different interests and backgrounds. This entails organizing and assisting powerless groups to become involved in determining their own future.

Policies, goals, and strategies of Metro Ministry are set by a board whose members are from the area served. Responsibility for implementing priorities is assigned to staff and task forces. Funding presently comes from the United Methodist Church at district, conference, and national levels.

Program areas of Metro Ministry include: criminal justice, camping for inner city youth, programs for low-income women, food co-ops, and policy issues in public education. As a result of these efforts, the Metro Ministry is very much involved with plans for a new county jail, inmate services, and the organization of a Police Practices Review Board. The camping program emphasizes the inclusion of minorities at all levels of camping—campers, staff, and camping committee—and a curriculum that meets the needs of minority campers. Programs and workshops for women have led to the formation of a Legal Aid Steering Committee which will use legal aid as the issue to involve low-income women. In the field of education, Metro Ministry has fought to have minority history taught in the public schools and is now organizing parents in a junior high school where suspension rates are high.

United Methodist pastors and lay members are very much a part of all aspects of Metro's ministry. The second Sunday in September is observed in 100 or more churches as "Metro Ministry Sunday," with the bulletin that day carrying a specially prepared insert outlining the Metro Ministry program.

Metro Ministry, 22 East Grand Avenue, Springfield, Ohio 45506. The Reverend John K. Waite, Director.

§

The Delta Ministry

The Delta Ministry in Greenville, Mississippi seeks to help the black and poor become aware of the issues that shape and/or influence their lives and actively involved in deciding how these issues will be resolved.

Motivation for action comes from a community education program consisting of forums on political, social, and economic issues. For instance, a forum on capital punishment resulted in The Delta Ministry working effectively with others in getting the number of death row prisoners reduced and in opposing the death penalty. A forum on compulsory school attendance led to working with residents of Greenville to establish a model Compulsory School Attendance Law that could serve other areas of the state if adopted. The Mississippi State Legislature has passed a very weak law which The Delta Ministry would like to see strengthened.

For several years, The Delta Ministry has provided financial and technical support to the Greenville Citizens for Representative Government. This group has sued to get Greenville to change its form of elections so city council members will be elected by wards rather than at large. A study is being made to see what affect the annexation of white communities into the city limits might have on the suit. The Delta Ministry is also working for legislative redistricting.

Though The Delta Ministry has many projects going at the same time, two are indicative of their outreach in service to the community. The first is a summer youth program held each year in memory of Mrs. Fannie Lou Hamer. This program has three components: historical research of the Civil Rights period, community services for the elderly on a one-to-one basis, and structured recreation. Seminars are held in conjunction with the Summer Youth Program.

The second is a demonstration hunger program to help the residents of Washington County identify economic alternatives to meet food and nutritional needs. As a model demonstration project, The Delta Ministry's Hunger Program combines and tests features of other hunger programs in seeking ways to feed "all" habitually hungry people regardless of race, age, religion, or physical condition.

The Delta Ministry, Box 457, Greenville, Mississippi 38701. Owen Brooks, Director. (50¢)

§

The Hunger Network in Ohio, Michigan, and Kentucky

The Hunger Network was activated in January 1978 after two years of planning, seeking support, and surveying church and community constituencies in Ohio. Nearly, 1,500 individuals indicated a willingness to be a part of a public policy organization to act in concert on national and state hunger issues. Funding was promised by United Methodists, United Presbyterians, and Episcopalians. Continued use of the Hunger Interest Survey increased membership rapidly, and a year later the Hunger Network expanded to include Michigan and Kentucky.

Through a variety of mailings and 15 newsletters a year, the Network informs members on the causes of hunger, theological approaches, legislative procedures, priority concerns, and action alerts. Address labels are coded to indicate the U.S. congressional district and the state senatorial and house district a person lives in.

On national and global issues, the Hunger Network relates to the National IMPACT Interreligious Task Force on U.S. Food Policy in Washington, D. C. At the state level, the Network works with state and local councils of churches, welfare rights groups, and citizen action agencies concerned about systemic changes related to hunger.

Between newsletters, the Hunger Network uses its well-organized telephone tree to alert members to take action. Each member receiving a call in turn calls six others. With computer print-outs quickly identifying members living in a specific district and the interests of those members, the telephone tree has become a very effective means of generating calls, letters, and telegrams to legislators when citizen action can count the most.

The Hunger Network in Ohio, Michigan, and Kentucky, 299 King Avenue, Columbus, Ohio 43201. Dr. Robert H. Bonthius, Director.

§

Energy Conservation Campaign

Initiated by the Interfaith Coalition on Energy (I.C.E.), The Energy Conservation Campaign seeks to encourage members of local churches to covenant together to conserve energy in a number of specific ways. (See page 60 of text for details.)

Interfaith Coalition on Energy, 236 Massachusetts Avenue, N. E., Washington, D. C. 20002. (25¢)

Green Community Services

This is an advocacy program funded by concerned churches—Congregational, Episcopal, and Roman Catholic—in Waterbury, Connecticut for two purposes: delivery of services to the needy and institutional change. Green Community Services is staffed by two Sisters of Notre de Namur.

Referrals to G.C.S. come from churches and institutions on the Green. Most needs can be taken directly to the social agencies responsible for providing those particular services. The Sisters interpret the benefits to which a person is entitled, help to cut the bureaucratic red tape, and follow through to see that services are delivered.

The direction of the program has often been determined by the problems confronted in securing services for clients. It has meant forming coalitions to work on specific issues. Legislators have been encouraged to support certain bills. Agencies have been urged to work more closely with other agencies and community groups. Welfare systems have been monitored to see that policies are applied uniformly and fairly. Changes have been suggested in the city welfare's clothing voucher policy and in the emergency food program. Workshops to educate the community have been developed with legal services.

The list of objectives and achievements indicates Green Community Services is effectively working to make social agencies responsive to the needs of the poor.

Green Community Services. The Reverend Herbert H. Mardis, 222 West Main Street, Waterbury, Connecticut 06702. ($1.00)

§

Children's Programs

1. Alaska Children's Services
2. Breakfast Program
3. Dental Clinic
4. Butterfly Childcare Center
5. Shelter Care Inn
6. CARING for children, inc.
7. Day Care Center
8. The Children's Clinic
9. Inner City Programs for Children

§

Alaska Children's Services

An ecumenical agency dedicated to serving the needs of troubled children and their families, Alaska Children's Services is an advocate for the welfare of children. It was founded in 1970.

Two of the first A.C.S. projects are now independent. One is the Center for Children and Parents, which developed specialized counseling services, play therapy, and parenting classes for abusive families. The other, the Iliuliuk Family and Health Services, was started as a pilot project in community organization and has become a model rural health and social services program. I.F.H.S. operates a health clinic, day-care center, and social services counseling program.

In the past few years, Alaska Children's Services has concentrated on providing quality emergency and residential care. Its Emergency Receiving Home provides crisis care for abused, neglected, and abandoned children. A Youth Services Center is a short-term crisis facility for 20 teenagers.

A.C.S. has also been involved with the construction of a new Activity Center to provide a needed gymnasium and classrooms at the Jesse Lee Home for children.

Several volunteers placed by church and ecumenical agencies assist the staff at A.C.S. facilities. Members of summer Work Camps contribute thousands of hours in painting and maintenance work.

Alaska Children's Services, 1200 East 27th Avenue, Anchorage, Alaska 99504. Dr. John Garvin, Executive Director.

Breakfast Program

This program is but one of many community services offered by Fellowship, Incorporated, the mission outreach arm of the East Topeka United Methodist Church.

A nourishing breakfast for children and youth is served every school day between 7:40 and 8:10 A.M. for a minimum charge of five cents—or five minutes of drying dishes. The pastor and church workers use this as a period for getting acquainted with the youth of the area, opening doors for counseling and guidance.

The salaries of the kitchen supervisor and several student assistants are provided by the Kansas East Conference of the United Methodist Church, but the actual program depends completely on donations and volunteer help.

The East Topeka United Methodist Church, a small inner-city congregation, has become known as "the church with soul in the heart of the city." Members continue to develop with Fellowship a program that combines Christian-oriented neighborhood service projects with the worship, study, and supportive fellowship of an established congregation. A clothes closet, a food cupboard, camp scholarships, a summer day camp, and help for approximately 250 families at Christmas are other Fellowship projects.

Fellowship, Incorporated, East Topeka United Methodist Church, 708 Lime, Topeka, Kansas 66607. The Reverend Gene Connely, Pastor-Director. (25¢)

§

Dental Clinic

The Shadow of the Church Ministry, the outreach program of the First United Methodist Church of Albuquerque, New Mexico, is providing a ministry to a number of area schools, most of which are located in socio-economically deprived neighborhoods.

Volunteers from the church congregation regularly assist dental hygienists by doing the clerical work and recording as students' teeth are checked. In one school alone, the Shadow of the Church Ministry distributed 500 toothbrushes last year as part of an educational program conducted by hygienists.

The church plans to continue this ministry as long as it is needed.

Shadow of the Church Ministry, First United Methodist Church. Write to Martha Hotchkiss, Coordinator of Inner-City Ministries, P.O. Box 1638, Albuquerque, New Mexico 87103.

Butterfly Childcare Center

The Turnagain United Methodist Church of Anchorage, Alaska long recognized the need for a nonprofit child-care facility in the community. Little was done about it, however, until the congregation was spurred to action by a few individuals who saw the church as the only building then large enough to accommodate such a program.

Plans moved forward, but the fire marshall refused to approve the classrooms and multipurpose area of the church as adequate for the number of children to be served. Not to be deterred, church members voted to use their sanctuary area for day care. Furniture was arranged for worship and weddings on weekends, but during the week the pews were removed.

The Butterfly Childcare Center operates a program for 40 children with an additional after-school program for about 15. Both the sanctuary and multipurpose area are used. Butterfly pays a minimum rent to offset utility costs, but has priority on use of the sanctuary space during the week. Butterfly provides custodial services for the areas it occupies, including the arranging of furniture as required by the dual use of the space.

Staff of the church and the Center work well together. The congregation has been represented on Butterfly's board of directors. After several years, the church and the Center are looking forward to a continued relationship.

Butterfly Childcare Center, Turnagain United Methodist Church, 3300 West Northern Lights Boulevard, Anchorage, Alaska 99503. Contact: William Trudeau or Lucie Stanton. (25¢)

§

Shelter Care Inn

The First Presbyterian Church of Upland, California opened a foster-care home in June 1974, with houseparents who had two small children of their own. In the first 18 months, 73 children between the ages of 1½ and 17½ were given 2,585 "child days" of care.

The children were referred to Shelter Care Inn by the Juvenile Division of San Bernardino County's Welfare Department. Church funds were used to establish the home and for repairs and furnishings. Members of the church provided appliances and equipment, clothing for the children, and babysitting for the houseparents. Church funds have not been needed for the general operation of this foster-care facility.

First Presbyterian Church, 869 N. Euclid Avenue, Upland, California 91786. The Reverend Richard Bunce.

CARING for children, inc.

CARING for children was established following a study of child-care needs by the Central United Methodist Church in Asheville, North Carolina.

The first project of CARING for children was an emergency shelter with residency of one to thirty days for children of any age who had no place to go. The facility used was a residence on the campus of Allen Center, a project of the United Methodist Board of Global Ministries. This shelter can house up to five children and has accommodated more than 200 children during the first three years of its existence.

A second home, opened in July 1978, houses up to five teenagers at a time without any restrictions as to length of residency. This home is cosponsored with the Children's Home of the Western North Carolina Annual Conference of the United Methodist Church located in Winston-Salem. The Western North Carolina Conference will provide a financial grant of $25,000 annually, and CARING for children will staff and manage the home.

CARING for children is operated by a board of directors consisting of persons from several denominations and churches, but with the majority of the members coming from Central United Methodist Church. Financial support comes through federal title grants, United Way, Central Church, and in smaller amounts from other interested individuals and groups.

Central United Methodist Church, 27 Church Street, Asheville, North Carolina 28801. Dr. Orion N. Hutchinson, Jr., Senior Minister. (Or Miss Linda Graney, Director, 331 College Street, Asheville, North Carolina 28801.)

§

Day Care Center

The congregation of First United Methodist Church in downtown Kenosha, Wisconsin sponsors a Day Care Center for children of working and/or single parents. Fees are kept low because the church assumes payment for all administrative costs and utilities. A staff of 15 supervises the 100 children enrolled. Lunch is served at noon to both teachers and children.

In addition to the full-day program, a before and after school program is available for public school children whose parents work.

Day Care Center, c/o Dr. Earl F. Lindsay, 919 60th Street, Kenosha, Wisconsin 53140.

The Children's Clinic

The Children's Clinic is a health care facility for sick children operated for two hours each Wednesday evening on the northside of Indianapolis. The Clinic is jointly sponsored by Second Presbyterian Church, the management of the Parc Chateau Apartments, and the Office of Community Health Nursing of the Health and Hospital Corporation of Marion County.

A well-baby clinic run by Community Health Nursing at the same facility on Wednesday mornings highlighted the need for sick child care. With funding unavailable for such a project, concerned individuals in Second Presbyterian Church created the Health Care Task Force to enlist community interest and volunteer staffing for a clinic.

Today, space for the Children's Clinic is furnished by the apartment management in two rent-free apartment units. Community Health Nursing provi , the malpractice insurance and a liaison nurse. The Health Care Task Force provides one doctor, two nurses (either R.N.'s or L.P.N.'s), one pediatric nurse practitioner (R.N.P.), and a receptionist each Wednesday evening. (More than 100 doctors, nurses, and receptionists have volunteered their time and services over a three-year period.) The Health Care Task Force has also been instrumental in collecting many of the drugs used in the Clinic as well as equipment and furnishings.

The Children's Clinic is a cooperative effort of the religious, private, and public sectors of the community to meet a specific need. None could provide this service alone, but together they make it possible for an average of 50 children to receive medical care weekly.

Health Care Task Force, Second Presbyterian Church, 7700 North Meridian Street, Indianapolis, Indiana 56260. The Reverend Verne E. Sindlinger.

§

Inner City Programs for Children

When eight downtown churches in Hartford, Connecticut organized Center City Churches, Inc., in 1967, their immediate concern was for the older residents of the city. However, through the years their outreach has touched all ages. Noteworthy are three programs for children: Children's City, Children's Theater, and Tutoring.

Children's City is focused on helping children see Hartford as an exciting city in which to live, to learn, and to have fun. The program takes place in various church buildings and involves about 100 children of elementary school age each summer. Daily sessions are held for six weeks. From the churches, the children move out each day into the spacious city parks, museums, commercial areas, etc. Rather than taking the children to the country to seek learning and enjoyment, Children's City affirms that Hartford offers this amply. A professional staff unites with high school and adult volunteers to provide the leadership for the program.

Children's Theater was started in the summer of 1974 as a multiracial, ecumenical theater workshop for children from five to fourteen years of age living in the Greater Hartford area. The purpose of the program is to help each child grow and develop self-confidence through participation in the performing arts. Two musicals a year have been presented, with each production having a cast of 35 to 40. All musicals are arranged so that each child will have a part of his or her own, thus affording a real feeling of pride and responsibility in the production.

Center City Churches, in late 1970, formed a structured *Tutorial* program for children who needed to build up their communication skills in reading and math. Children from two schools have participated in the program through the years with high school students, senior citizens, and other concerned adults tutoring on a one-to-one basis each week.

Center City Churches, Inc., 170 Main Street, Hartford, Connecticut 06106.

§

Criminal Justice/Prison Ministries

1. Pre-Trial Support Project
2. Rochester Interfaith Jail Ministry
3. County Prison Education/Seminar Program
4. Project 60
5. Monroe Alternatives Project (M.A.P.)
6. Criminal Justice Ministry
7. Ministry of Criminal Justice

§

Pre-Trial Support Project

The Des Moines Area Urban Mission Council of the United Methodist Church launched the Pre-Trial Support Project after surveys indicated hundreds of persons were languishing in Iowa jails while awaiting trial for only one reason—they were poor. Even when eligible for bond, they were unable to raise the funds for their release.

Of the 52 clients released during the first five months of the Pre-Trial Support Project, 45 were women. Most had been charged during a time of economic crisis that had led them to turn to shoplifting, check writing, prostitution, etc., in an attempt to provide for their dependents.

In almost all cases, clients are referred by the courts onrecognizance in lieu of previously stated bond. The few who have taken flight to avoid prosecution have been found and delivered back to court custody.

A summary of cases for an 18-month period indicates that most of the cases legitimately before the courts involved property crimes symptomatic of unemployment and living costs. In response, the Pre-Trial Support Project has endeavored to help clients find employment, housing, food and clothing. It has provided assistance in solving family problems and improving the quality of the environment. It has encouraged self-sufficiency and avoidance of future difficulty with the law.

The Pre-Trial Support Project has also monitored and advocated changes in the criminal justice process. It has urged the community to provide alternatives to incarceration of the poor through preventive action in areas of employment, economic support and community environment.

The Pre-Trial Support Project is directed by one paid employee, who is assisted by concerned citizens belonging to a number of community organizations and religious bodies. A small task force deals with policy decisions on behalf of the sponsoring Urban Mission Council.

Criminal Outreach/Justice Project (formerly Pre-Trial Support Project), Des Moines Area Urban Mission Council, 921 Pleasant Street, Des Moines, Iowa 50309. The Reverend Ken Fineran, Urban Minister.

§

Rochester Interfaith Jail Ministry

This ministry is the response of churches and synagogues in Monroe County, New York to the needs of the 6,000 or more persons detained each year for at least one night in the county jail while awaiting trial.

Volunteer visitors, both clergy and lay persons, are given training by the Rochester Interfaith Jail Ministry in such areas as legal procedures, counseling, and available community resources. A "Guide for Volunteers" is presented to each individual completing the training.

In addition to providing support to the prison visitors, the two full-time staff persons serve as advocates for prisoners wishing to file complaints. The Rochester Interfaith Jail Ministry staff, working closely with the Judicial Process Commission of the Genesee Ecumenical Ministries and other community groups, has been involved in the investigation of jail conditions conducted by the Grand Jury and State Commission of Correction. R.I.J.M. also initiated meetings to examine and address the serious suicide problem in the county jail.

The Rochester Interfaith Jail Ministry serves the community at large by increasing public awareness of the problems of the judicial system, particularly regarding jails and prisons. A slide show has been developed and speakers are provided for religious and community groups and schools.

Funding for staff salaries and training programs comes from contributions of churches, synagogues, and individuals. Policies are set and the ministry program coordinated by a board whose members represent major religious bodies and minority groups. An ex-inmate serves on the board to be sure that concerns of prisoners are understood and considered.

Rochester Interfaith Jail Ministry, Inc., 101 Plymouth Avenue South, Rochester, New York 14608. Robert E. Bonn, Executive Director. (25¢) The "Guide for Volunteers" is available for $1.00.

§

County Prison Education/Seminar Program

The Social Ministry Committee of the Holy Trinity Lutheran Church in Lancaster, Pennsylvania has been active in providing programs for the inmates of the Lancaster County Prison. Through the work of this committee a "bestseller of the month" program for the prison library has been provided, and a series of mini-courses for incarcerated women has been started. These classes, taught by church members, deal with such practical skills as home budgeting, job applications, and first aid. In addition, one-to-one help is being given in reading, mathematics, and English grammar by volunteer tutors.

Holy Trinity Lutheran Church, 31 South Duke Street, Lancaster, Pennsylvania 17602. The Reverend B. Penrose Hoover, Pastor.

§

Project 60

Project 60 was started in 1973 as a joint venture of the Pennsylvania Council of Churches and the Pennsylvania Bureau of Corrections with the initial funding coming from the Pennsylvania Office for the Aging. Today, Project 60 is the major program of Consilium, Inc., a nonprofit private organization bringing together government agencies, private resources, the church, and business. The Pennsylvania Council of Churches and the Pennsylvania Catholic Conference continue to be actively interested and involved.

Project 60 operates as an agent independent of the prison system and government to provide services to elderly offenders and ex-offenders, with the aim of successful resocialization. A statewide program, it offers consultation, therapy, counseling, education, and service to inmates of Pennsylvania Correctional Institutions who are 59 years of age or older and anticipating release. These same services are continued after release until an individual chooses to operate independently. Project 60 also provides advocacy and assistance to make release possible.

Of those who have been released under this program, no client has reentered an institution as a result of a criminal offense. This is significant in that most of the clients were previously chronic recidivists. Those who were alcoholics or convicted of alcohol-related crimes have not returned to problematic drinking. Twenty-five percent are now employed in the community and are proving to be reliable, steady workers.

The successes of Project 60 are seen not only in the rehabilitation of its clients and their positive reentry into society, but also in the obvious contribution to the criminal justice system at a time when incarceration is estimated to cost at least $10,000 per year and more for the elderly and their special medical needs.

Project 60 counselors spend approximately 53% of their time in direct contact with their clients. Another 20% is spent in dealing with the institutions and community services on behalf of clients. The remainder of their time is devoted to travel and to staff training and development, a continuing crucial aspect of the program.

Other states have expressed interest in Project 60, and it has become the model for a pilot project now operating in West Virginia.

Project 60, Consilium, Inc., 500 North Main Street, Room 105, Pittsburgh, Pennsylvania 15215. Mrs. Jane C. Burger, Program Administrator.

§

Monroe Alternatives Project (M.A.P.)

The Monroe Alternatives Project of the Judicial Process Commission, Genesee Ecumenical Ministries, seeks to identify problem areas in the criminal justice system of Monroe County, New York, and then to find possible solutions. The following blueprint for action has been devised:

Before trial
— Legislatively reduce the number of criminal categories.
— Implement procedures for referral to mental health and sobering-up centers.
— Except for serious felonies, expand the use of appearance tickets.
— Train police in stress reduction tactics for family crisis situations.
— Establish crisis housing for troubled youth.
— Expand the use of pre-trial release and diversion programs.
— Utilize mediation and arbitration programs instead of arrest and jail to resolve interpersonal conflicts.

After trial
— Improve and expand probation services.
— Require restitution to injured parties and the community.
— Expand work, education, job-training programs.
— Establish halfway houses as sentencing and/or release options.
— Reduce the number of cells in the county jail as alternatives affect jail population.

Monroe Alternatives Project of the Judicial Process Commission, 101 Plymouth Avenue South, Rochester, New York 14608. Diane Larter, Coordinator. (50¢)

Criminal Justice Ministry

This ministry is a cooperative venture of the Memphis Presbytery of the Presbyterian Church, U.S. through its Urban Outreach Commission, and of the Catholic Diocese of Memphis. Volunteers are recruited, trained, and assigned to work in various areas of the Memphis criminal justice system. Some work directly with prisoners, others relate to the families of prisoners, and still others are working with prison officials.

The program began in the spring of 1978 and by early fall had 85 volunteers trained and placed. A budget of $22,000 provides for a staff of one full-time person and three part-time workers.

There are hopes of expanding this program to include other denominations.

Urban Commission, First Presbyterian Church, 166 Poplar, Memphis, Tennessee 38103. The Reverend Jack M. White.

§

Ministry of Criminal Justice

Begun in 1975, the Ministry of Criminal Justice was incorporated as a private nonprofit organization two years later under the direction of the Illinois United Methodist Church and funded by the Law Enforcement Assistance Administration through the Illinois Law Enforcement Commission. Financial contributions have also come from the three annual conferences of the United Methodist Church in Illinois, the Illinois Department of Corrections, and private gifts.

The Ministry of Criminal Justice has two components or projects. The first, C.U.P. or Communities Upholding Persons, is a statewide effort to recruit and train volunteers to work in local jails and state prisons. Their goal is to establish relationships with offenders, ex-offenders, and their families. (See page 57 of text for more information on C.U.P.)

The second component, E.G.O. or Educational Growth Opportunities, advances the proposition that social responsibility can exist only with personal responsibility. It proposes that each person should be helped to understand his/her role and obligation in life. This is done through educational and human growth experiences for correctional center residents in groups of 15. The course provides 160 hours of classroom work.

Illinois United Methodist Church Ministry of Criminal Justice, Inc., 3801 North Keeler Avenue, Chicago, Illinois 60641. The Reverend William G. Johnson, Executive Director. ($1.00)

Disaster Relief Programs

1. Sponsorship/Resettlement of a Refugee Family
2. Mission to Wilkes-Barre
3. Teton Interfaith Disaster Task Force
4. Disaster Preparedness

§

Sponsorship/Resettlement of a Refugee Family

The First United Methodist Church of Centralia, Washington is just one of many churches across the country that has undertaken the sponsorship of a refugee family from Southeast Asia. Because of their good experience, members have offered direct assistance as consultants to other sponsors.

First Church made its application through the United Methodist Committee for Overseas Relief and Church World Service and was assigned a married couple with a son from Laos.

Looking back after a year, church members felt they had fulfilled the terms of their contract and far more. The family had been met at the airport and provided housing. Both the husband and wife had been assisted in finding employment and in adjusting to community life. The couple had been enrolled in English classes with church volunteers offering additional tutoring three times a week. Other volunteers repaired and painted the house rented for the family. Still others assisted with filling out forms, going with the family as necessary until adjusted to American life, and providing moral support all along the way.

The couple have responded well and have, in turn, offered a helping hand to several other refugee families in the area.

For information, write to *Mrs. William Lawrence,* Coordinator of the project, at 905 Spring Lane, Centralia, Washington 98531.

Church World Service, National Council of Churches, 475 Riverside Drive, New York, New York 10115.

§

Mission to Wilkes-Barre

Following hurricane Agnes in 1972, Wilkes-Barre, Pennsylvania was flooded for a five-mile radius on both sides of the Susquehanna River. This devastating flood ripped some houses from their foundations and covered others with a coat of gray mud. Churches and commercial properties had to be reconstructed.

Concerned members of the First United Methodist Church in Hyattsville, Maryland contacted William and Margaret Reid, pastors of Central United Methodist Church in Wilkes-Barre, to offer their help, particularly in restoring the church. The Mission to Wilkes-Barre project was born. In the two years of its existence, workers willing to share skills and time were recruited from several United Methodist churches. They were asked for one or more weekends and, because of the advance planning of the project director with the Reids, specific tasks.

Teams of 10 to 50 persons were made up of secretaries, carpenters, painters, electricians, plumbers, upholsterers, and others willing to shovel debris, scrub, and cook for the group in an improvised kitchen. Participants brought their own tools and paid a $5.00 fee each trip to cover the cost of food and supplies for repair projects. They also took along sleeping bags and cots.

Some workers were in their early teens; some were in their 70s. There was, however, no generation gap as they shouldered together jobs that were often dirty and exhausting. Saturday nights were fun times with such group activities as square dancing. The spirit of the teams was phenomenal and led to many in the group returning time and again.

As some of the Wilkes-Barre people completed the cleaning and restoration of their own homes, they began working weekends alongside the Marylanders. A beautiful relationship developed between the two peoples. On one occasion, the Wilkes-Barre church prepared a sumptuous dinner for the visiting group. Later, they journeyed to Maryland for a weekend of sightseeing and fellowship with their new friends.

Perhaps more important than the hours of labor was the emotional support offered by the Maryland church members in the name of Christ to people beaten down with adversity. A bond was established between the two communities that will continue to exist for many years to come.

The project director of Mission to Wilkes-Barre was the wife of the pastor of First United Methodist Church in Hyattsville at the time. Her present address is given below.

Ms. Nan Doggett, Project Director, Mission to Wilkes-Barre, 131 – 2nd Street, Frederick, Maryland 21701.

Teton Interfaith Disaster Task Force

This ecumenical task force was quickly organized following the 1976 Teton Dam disaster that left many communities in eastern Idaho flooded. Closely allied with the Ecumenical Association of Churches in Idaho, the Teton Interfaith Disaster Task Force worked cooperatively with the Red Cross, Church World Service, and other relief agencies in establishing needed services in the stricken areas.

Volunteers were immediately enlisted to help with the cleanup. At least 250 persons were trained as grief counselors to work on a one-to-one basis with those who had lost jobs, homes, etc. Thousands of sandwiches were made and distributed daily. Family-to-family support groups were formed.

The Teton Interfaith Disaster Task Force, in existence 13 months, counted among its achievements:

- —Legal assistance for the flood victims by offering state officials office space, secretarial service, and a telephone.
- —An initial disaster mental health grant that supplied ten social workers by providing from its records the supporting data needed by the federal government.
- —$10,000 for summer camp scholarships so all youth in areas where recreational facilities had been destroyed could have an opportunity for recreation.
- —A long-term recreation program for several communities by sharing in the planning with state, county, and public school leaders and by obtaining and installing used playground equipment in three of the communities.
- —A Christmas vacation recreation program in the public schools by arranging for supervision and transportation money.
- —A home repair program by agreeing to supply materials if the state would make CETA funds available for the salaries of those hired to do the work. All workers received sufficient training and experience to qualify for construction jobs when the home repair program came to an end. More than 500 homes were repaired.

And the list goes on. The Teton Interfaith Disaster Task Force worked directly with local, state, and federal agencies in giving assistance wherever it was needed.

Teton Interfaith Disaster Task Force information is available from its Executive Director: *Marvin Eld,* P. O. Box 1136, Idaho Falls, Idaho 83401. $1.00

Disaster Preparedness

Several years ago the Associated Churches of Fort Wayne and Allen County in Indiana held a Disaster Consultation to which each church and synagogue was invited to send two representatives.

The purpose was to see how well religious institutions could respond in an emergency. A survey was made to find out which congregations had clothing banks and food pantries and how many people could be accommodated for feeding and sleeping in each building in case of a tornado or other disaster.

Representatives attending the consultation were asked to serve as coordinators in their own congregations for enlisting volunteers and planning procedures.

The Red Cross cooperated in this effort and later conducted training sessions on feeding, housing, counseling of victims, cleanup, and repair work. Forms, available for churches to sign, not only authorized the Red Cross to use facilities but spelled out financial arrangements.

The Associated Churches, 6430 Upper Huntington Road, Fort Wayne, Indiana 46804. Melvin R. Phillips, Executive Director.

§

Education/Information Programs

1. Brooklyn Information Center
2. Alternatives, Inc.
3. Community Intern Program
4. Possibility Book
5. Public Dialogue Series
6. Volunteer Interfaith Program
7. Education Resource Network
8. Seminars on National and International Affairs

§

Brooklyn Information Center

Miseries of countless numbers of low-income and minority groups are compounded by ignorance of existing community services available to them. This is particularly true in sprawling urban areas such as Brooklyn, New York. Many federal, state, city, and privately funded agencies operate on stringent budgets allowing little or no allocations for publicity of their services. People live, fall ill, and often die unaware of the existence of a health clinic a few blocks away offering free diagnosis and treatment. They fail to realize that there are job-training programs, employment agencies, and other social-welfare groups waiting to serve them.

The United Interfaith Action Council of Brooklyn, Inc. acts as a clearinghouse for all pertinent information related to the major areas of concern affecting the daily lives of the poor. Specific information (names, addresses, and telephone numbers) for services offered by city, state, federal, and private agencies is compiled, reproduced, and made available to churches, other agencies, and individuals upon request.

United Interfaith Action Council of Brooklyn, Inc., 268 Stuyvesant Avenue, Brooklyn, New York 11221. Claire Robertson, Executive Director. (50¢)

§

Alternatives, Inc.

In the fall of 1973 a church activist, Bob Kochtitzky, published a 60-page paperback with the intriguing title *Alternate Christmas Catalogue*. This was one man's response to the increasing commercialism of Christmas, birthdays, and other special occasions. The catalogue urged the return to a simpler lifestyle and a more meaningful observance of holidays. It suggested that funds saved be directed to organizations supporting worthy causes.

The idea caught hold. Church denominations provided grants for the producing of a second Christmas catalogue in 1974 and resource packets on alternate celebrations for other special days. A quarterly newsletter was begun. A mail-order service was established, offering a wide range of publications dealing with alternative lifestyles, celebrations, and economic and social change.

Two more catalogues have been published, each receiving considerable media coverage. A National Alternative Celebrations Campaign has been launched to enlist 1,000 study/action groups in the promotion of the Alternatives concepts. The *Voluntary Simplicity Study-Action Guide* prepared for the use of these groups offers 12 study-sessions on Christmas, Valentine's Day, Easter, funerals, weddings, Independence Day, etc., with action suggestions.

Today there is a vast network of people calling for others to examine their lifestyles and consumption habits. More than a million dollars has been diverted to solve problems of world hunger and other human needs.

Alternatives, Box 429, Ellenwood, Georgia 30049.

§

Community Intern Program

This program is designed to provide direct services to the metropolitan community of Portland, Oregon, while assisting in the training of persons interested in community service as a career. Funding comes from the benevolence budget of the First United Methodist Church.

The program began with the hiring of one intern and has expanded over a twelve-year period so that six interns are now being hired each year. Interns are carefully selected through an established screening process. They need not be members of the church. Many are college students working for the summer, but other adults, including retired senior citizens and persons with professional degrees, have also been chosen. Interests of the applicants are matched with programs of public-service agencies. The period of employment ranges from three months to a year and can be either full-time or part-time.

While employed, the intern is under the direction of the agency. The church does ask that each one provide a short written or oral report indicating how people in need were served.

More than 25 local service agencies have participated and been aided by this program. Some of these were well-established agencies; others have been innovative ministries. Thus, interns have had the opportunity to work in a variety of community-action programs and rehabilitation projects.

The First United Methodist Church, 1838 S.W. Jefferson, Portland Oregon 97201. Contact person: Max D. Pew, Lay Associate. (50¢)

§

Possibility Book

All too often it takes a crisis situation for adults to realize that they do not know where to turn for help or what services are available to them. A person does not have to be "poor" to need or to receive help.

This realization led the Social Concerns Commission of the Broadway United Methodist Church in Orlando, Florida to publish the *Possibility Book,* a compilation of organizations and services available in the metropolitan Orlando area. This 40-page book is carefully indexed with 19 different types of services listed. Some of these services are regrouped on an additional page for those needing special transportation, help morally and spiritually during a period of terminal illness in the family, and guidance and help at a time of death.

Page headings are easily read, and the information for each service includes its purpose, address, hours available, telephone number, fees (if any), and program. The name of the director or contact person is also provided.

In addition, the Social Concerns Commission lists four committees of three persons each that can be called at any hour for immediate assistance in time of crisis. These names with phone numbers are printed opposite the table of contents.

The back cover of the book lists the police and fire emergency numbers for Orlando and surrounding areas.

Broadway/Concord Park United Methodist Church, 406 East Amelia Street, Orlando, Florida 32803. The Reverend Ken Crossman, Minister.

§

Public Dialogue Series

In 1978 the Syracuse Area Interreligious Council, the membership of which includes representatives from the Jewish, Roman Catholic, and Protestant communities, initiated a series of dialogues on critical issues facing citizens of the city and county.

All topics are chosen because of their complexity and the controversy surrounding them. For instance, the first three dealt with: (1) a solid waste disposal crisis; (2) the question to rebuild, or not rebuild, the Jamesville Penitentiary; and (3) the matter of a city-suburban student exchange program to provide integration in the schools. All issues are ones on which citizens need to be well informed if they are to act wisely and to exert influence before decisions are made.

Panelists are key leaders representing the varying sides of the subject for discussion. Members of the Syracuse Area Interreligious Council serve as moderators. Audience participation is encouraged during the question and answer periods. All sessions are held in a convenient location, the Parish House of the First Presbyterian Church, for noontime attendance. Each dialogue runs for an hour and a half. Brown-bag lunches are brought and eaten as individuals listen. Coffee and tea are served.

Publicity for the series has included a newsletter, "S.A.I.C.'s Alive," which gives the history, background, and points of concern on the topic for discussion that month. Its wide distribution, general press coverage, and community response indicate continued interest in the dialogue series.

Public Dialogue Series, Syracuse Area Interreligious Council, 910 Madison Street, Syracuse, New York 13210. Dorothy F. Rose, Executive Director. Jean Graybeal, Editor of "S.A.I.C.'s Alive."

§

Volunteer Interfaith Program

Extended Hand, Inc., formed by churches and service groups initially to work in the field of subsidized housing in Silver Spring, Maryland, voted in late 1976 to shift the emphasis of the organization's activities to adult education through the Volunteer Interfaith Program. Available volunteer resources would be concentrated on teaching low-income families and new arrivals from foreign countries how to cope with the complexities of urban living.

Nearly 200 enrolled for the V.I.P. classes in the spring of 1977. Students came from about 35 different countries. Two-thirds were learning conversational English. The rest were studying basic education or preparing to take high school equivalency exams. About 30 students were taking typing and eight were preparing for Civil Service tests.

Fall enrollment exceeded 200, necessitating the placing of some prospective students on a waiting list. All available space at the Clifton Park Baptist Church was being utilized and classes were larger than desirable. Three new teachers were recruited and the Silver Spring Presbyterian Church opened some of its classrooms, so by October all on the waiting list had been accommodated.

The Volunteer Interfaith Program functions, according to the 1977 annual report, "because approximately 100 people in the community have enough concern for their neighbors to devote a few hours each week to some aspect of the program. V.I.P. requires not only teachers, but also drivers, nursery teachers, a 'kitchen crew' for the coffee break, and individuals to plan and coordinate the overall effort. Altogether, the time contributed by these volunteers would cost well over $50,000 per year at commercial rates . . . something between $130 and $150 per student per semester."

Nursery care for preschoolers and a well-developed transportation system are crucial to the success of the Volunteer Interfaith Program. Nursery teachers prepare toddlers for Head Start or kindergarten. Care is also included for infants, a service greatly appreciated by many young mothers who lose little time from classes when new babies arrive. Coffee breaks are used by some for breast-feeding their babies.

Coordinating the 41 carpools necessary to provide transportation for all who need it proved to be very time consuming early in the program. This task has now been taken over by a group of retirees from Marvin Memorial United Methodist Church, who have an effective system working. Three carpools of students are brought in from a nearby neighborhood where there is a great need for a similar adult education program but where a sufficient number of volunteers has not yet been cultivated.

A special characteristic of all programs initiated by Extended Hand, Inc., is the extension by volunteers of a personal "hand up" to those being served. Person-to-person relationships are rewarding for both volunteers and students in the Volunteer Interfaith Program. Successes outweigh the disappointments.

Volunteer Interfaith Program, c/o Eleanor E. Widman, 1606 Wilson Place, Silver Spring, Maryland 20910.

§

Education Resource Network

In response to a survey of school-related community organizations in Rochester, New York, the Genesee Ecumenical Ministries established the Educational Resource Network to provide the communication, information, and mutual support needed among these groups. Operation began in 1975 with the help of a federal grant under the Emergency School Aid Act.

The stated purpose of the Education Resource Network is "to develop within a neutral setting effective community support for the public schools of Rochester so that the highest quality and equality of educational opportunities for all children will be assured." E.R.N. is based on the belief that the closer the tie between schools and community the more responsive schools can be to the emerging needs of children, and the greater the resource the community can be in the educational process.

E.R.N. maintains a link between educational needs and resources in the community through a monthly newsletter and a resource bank. *The Network* is published and distributed without cost to over 600 local groups, community leaders, and educators. This newsletter provides a forum through which significant educational issues are researched and reported. It also acts as a "Want Ads" service for everyone interested in the city schools where information, ideas, projects, problems, needs, and resources can be shared.

The Resource Bank gathers and catalogs information on school-related student, parent, and community organizations, projects, skills, research reports, periodicals, etc. Anyone with an interest, question, or concern about Rochester public education can use the services of the Resource Bank. Questions, for instance, might relate to standardized tests, open enrollment, educational alternatives for senior highs, classroom discipline, career orientation programs available through local industries, and even fund-raising ideas.

Both the newsletter and the Resource Bank depend greatly upon the help of volunteers for reporting, researching, writing, cataloging, typing, and general office work.

Education Resource Network. Genesee Ecumenical Ministries, 50 North Plymouth Avenue, Rochester, New York 14614. William J. Benet, Director.

§

Seminars on National and International Affairs

Many denominational offices in Washington and New York are prepared to help groups of high school youth, college students, and adults examine social issues and legislative processes from a Christian perspective.

The authors of this book are especially familiar with the United Methodist Seminars on National and International Affairs, a program operated jointly by the Board of Church and Society and the Women's Division, Board of Global Ministries. With a design team in Washington and another in New York, the seminar program recognizes that national and international issues are related. Seminar participants thus evaluate national priorities in light of international responsibility.

Though these seminars are a part of the educational program of the United Methodist Church, they emphasize the need for Christian involvement in the pressing issues of the nation and the world.

Reservations for a seminar in either Washington or New York, or in both cities, should be made well in advance. Group leaders will be expected to coordinate housing, transportation, and sightseeing plans; the seminar design team will arrange for speakers, literature, conference rooms, etc. The cost of a seminar depends on the size of the group and the number of days spent in study.

United Methodist Seminars on National and International Affairs, 100 Maryland Avenue, N.E., Washington, D.C. 20002 and 777 United Nations Plaza, Room 800, New York, New York 10017.

§

Health and Counseling Programs

1. Koinonia Medical Center
2. Counseling Service and Help Lines
3. Free Clinic
4. The Yule Connection
5. The Pastoral Counseling Center
6. Ministry to the Deaf
7. Night Ministry
8. Women's Refuge, Inc.
9. Health Fair
10. Hearing Aid Bank
11. Matthew 25 Health Clinic

§

Koinonia Medical Center

This health care facility in Muskegon Heights, Michigan is devoted to serving those financially unable to afford the cost of a physician and other medical services. (See page 55 of text.)

Physical examinations and follow-ups are done by physician assistants with a pediatric nurse doing most of the checkups on babies and children. Six doctors, each giving one-half day a week, are responsible for all diagnostic decisions, treatment of the acutely ill, and office surgery.

The only persons ever turned away from the Center are those whose income or insurance coverage places them above the eligibility standards. These patients are referred to other doctors.

Many community organizations and resource groups cooperate with Koinonia Medical Center in providing the medically indigent with full professional services and counseling.

Koinonia Medical Center, 780 Hovey, Muskegon Heights, Michigan 49444. The Reverend Ben Ypma, Pastoral Counselor. ($1.00)

§

Counseling Service and Help Lines

These are but two of some rather innovative programs established by the Rural Community Action Ministry (RCAM) serving Androscoggin, Kennebec, and Oxford Counties in Maine. RCAM attempts to bring services —pastoral, health, social, and economic—to where people live. Financial support comes from over fifteen area churches, various denominations, local organizations and businesses, and interested individuals.

The RCAM Counseling Service Committee, with the assistance of a professional mental-health consultant, is actively involved in promoting community mental-health education. In 1977, workshops were held on Family Relations, Child Abuse (to train volunteers to assist in homes where this is a problem), and Helping Families and Children Cope with Divorce. The five areas of service offered by this committee are:

- —Mental health information and referral;
- —Marriage, family, and individual counseling through Tri-County Mental Health Services;
- —Training volunteers to handle mental-health crises, organize Help Lines, work with the elderly;
- —Consultation and training for ministers;
- —Mental-health education programs.

Help Lines are established in five towns in the area. This is a telephone service with numbers people can call in a time of crisis and when desiring prayer. Trained volunteers provide these services and also call shut-ins and senior citizens on a regular basis.

Rural Community Action Ministry, Franciscan Monastery, Greene, Maine 04236.

§

Free Clinic

The Second Baptist Church of Los Angeles, California operates a free clinic the last Saturday of every month. Blood pressure readings, urinalysis, blood tests, eye examinations, and tests for sickle cell anemia are conducted by physicians from the Charles R. Drew Postgraduate Medical School.

The initiative to establish the clinic came from the Community Relations Commission of the church and interested persons at Drew School. Leadership continues to be shared.

Free Clinic, Mr. Nate George, 4859 Parkglen, Los Angeles, California 90043. (25¢)

The Yule Connection

It was mid-November, 1977, when the Church Federation of Greater Chicago conceived the idea of a twenty-four-hour Christmas phone hotline to remain open from noon on December 23 until midnight, December 28.

The purpose was defined:" . . . to connect persons in the metropolitan area with programs and projects which need them, to provide a place for special involvement during this most special of times, at the same time it is designed to provide an avenue for those who are lonely and isolated to be in caring contact with other people." Through the Yule Connection it was hoped that many might be helped to overcome the worst aspects of the depression, loneliness, and sadness often associated with holidays.

The pressure of time made the job difficult. Responsibilities were divided to cover:

—recruiting and training volunteers for the phones.
—compiling a list of organizations, agencies, and persons to whom callers could be referred.
—planning and implementing an extensive publicity campaign.
—coordinating the entire effort.

Volunteers emerged from far beyond the Chicago metropolitan area to cover the phones and to offer the necessary backup services. Over 130 people attended the three-and-one-half-hour training session offered to acquaint them with referral resources and procedures to be followed in crisis situations.

Those gathering information on agencies discovered that many would not be open during part or all of the period. Hours and names of contact persons were carefully noted. Organizations offering food, clothing, and toys were listed. The idea was to avoid "blind referrals."

The communications staff of the Federation received full support of the media. Television and radio stations used public service announcements and prerecorded spots prepared by the communications committee. Yule Connection participants appeared on numerous talk shows. Newspapers throughout the area carried the story. The Chicago Daily News even became a "co-architect" of the project. Major wire services carried the Yule Connection story nationally.

During the Christmas period, the Church Federation of Greater Chicago sponsored several programs on TV and radio that would speak to those uninvolved with family and friends.

Over 1,400 calls were received by the Yule Connection. They came from every part of the metropolitan area, with 22% from persons still in their 20s and 25% from those 60 and over. Some callers desired to share themselves with others. The lonely had responded with both social and physical needs.

Detailed records were kept and a complete report issued by the Church Federation in the spring.

The Church Federation of Greater Chicago, 116 South Michigan Avenue, Chicago, Illinois 60603.

§

The Pastoral Counseling Center

Many cities now have counseling centers with an ecumenical staff of professional counselors and with a number of churches and denominational agencies offering support. These centers provide a skilled counseling service to supplement the ministry of local pastors. It recognizes and, when appropriate, utilizes the religious dimension of a person's life in the counseling process without imposing any particular religious framework.

The Pastoral Counseling Center of the Genesee Ecumenical Ministries in Rochester, New York is very similar to others over the country but one that could well serve as a model.

Staff of the Rochester Center counsel with individuals, marriage partners, and family groups without regard for race or religious preference. Fees for counseling sessions are on a sliding scale depending upon income, family size, and other circumstances. Arrangements can be made for the sessions to take place in any one of eight or more locations (churches) scattered over the city so that transportation need not be a problem.

The Rochester Center staff also provides professional seminars for ministers, training in several fields for church groups, and educational programs for adults. Themes for the clergy seminars have been: Ministry to the Bereaved, Premarital Counseling, Ministry to the Aging, Marriage Counseling, and Counseling Case Study.

Church groups have welcomed training in lay calling and visitation, lay counseling, and conflict management. Adult programs have dealt with such subjects as contemporary family problems, self-worth and self-defeat, human sexuality, how to handle bereavement, marriage enrichment, and how to face life tasks (work, friendship, marriage, and spirituality).

The Pastoral Counseling Center, Genesee Ecumenical Ministries Office, 17 South Fitzhugh Street, Rochester, New York 14614. The Reverend John Karl, Executive Counselor.

§

Ministry to the Deaf

For more than twenty years the congregation of the Riverside Christian Church in Wichita, Kansas has included 40 to 50 deaf members. Though those with hearing handicaps have their own church school class and study group, they share in worship services and other activities with someone interpreting in sign language. Deaf members have served in many different leadership roles, including that of deacon. Recently one was elected an elder.

Members of the deaf group participate as lay leaders in the worship services and, once a year, take charge of an entire service. On these occasions, someone interprets for the hearing community. The deaf have their own choir and make many outside appearances.

Riverside Church has a telephone-teletypewriter machine in the church office and provides any member who desires one with a machine for home use. This enables the deaf to keep in touch with each other as well as with the church.

Both hearing and nonhearing members of the church have had their lives enriched by their shared experiences.

Riverside Christian Church, 1001 Litchfield, Wichita, Kansas 67203. The Reverend Gerald Waters, Minister. (25¢)

§

Night Ministry

The San Francisco Council of Churches claims to have the longest continuing night ministry of its kind. Trained lay volunteers provide a listening ear as well as counseling for individuals in crisis who call the Night Ministry between 10:00 P.M. and 4:00 A.M. any night of the year. In addition, an ordained minister walks the streets of San Francisco during the same hours, available to any one in need no matter where the circumstances of their lives may have led them. The Night Minister can be reached by the lay volunteers through an electronic beeper, thus making it possible to serve the entire city.

The Night Ministry has a Director of Volunteers who screens applicants for the telephone operation and then schedules the volunteers for their once- or twice-a-month service. Special advance training is supplemented with in-service training as needed to assure a competent staff.

The Night Minister has a staff of six Assistant Night Ministers with one available each night to respond to calls for help. A 1977 report indicates there were 4,271 such calls that year. Lay volunteers served an equal number of persons. In addition, 653 persons received emergency housing and 233 were given food.

The Night Ministry is funded by four denominations from a regional or jurisdictional area: Lutheran Church Missouri Synod, Protestant Episcopal Church, Lutheran Church in America, and the American Baptist Churches of the West. Many churches and individuals have participated in the program.

San Francisco Council of Churches, 944 Market Street, San Francisco, California 94102.

§

Women's Refuge, Inc.

Women's Refuge is one of the newest projects of the Interfaith Consortium for Community Action of Greater Cumberland, an association of churches and organizations in western Maryland.

Developed through the efforts of lay, professional, and religious leaders, Women's Refuge provides temporary shelter, supportive counseling, and appropriate referral if longer-term counseling is advisable. It also hopes to improve community understanding of the problem of wife abuse.

Services are available to physically and/or emotionally abused women, including those who are destitute and transient. All client information is kept completely confidential.

Housed in the Community Counseling Center, the Refuge is open to all women who need its services during normal working hours Monday through Friday. Emergency service is available at any hour, including holidays and weekends, when the referral is made through law enforcement agencies, hospitals, Social Services, the Health Department, or Hotline.

There are no mandatory fees. However, clients are encouraged to reimburse the Refuge at a time when their financial situation permits.

CETA funding made it possible to employ a professional to direct the program in its beginning stages. Volunteer assistants were trained in a series of workshops conducted by the Allegany County Association for Mental Health and the Community Services Office at Allegany Community College.

Women's Refuge, Inc., Seton Plaza, Suite 201, 952 Seton Drive, Cumberland, Maryland 21502.

§

Health Fair

The Lakeside Elder Adult Project and the Allen County Council on Aging in Fort Wayne, Indiana sponsored a five-hour health fair for senior citizens that proved to provide all that the title promised: "Everything you always wanted to know about health but were afraid to ask because it might cost too much."

During the hours of 10:00 A.M. to 3:00 P.M., visitors to the fair could visit 40 different booths and have an inexpensive lunch of soup, sandwich, homemade cookies, and drink served by the ladies of the Crescent Avenue United Methodist Church, where the fair was held.

In addition to having blood pressure, height, and weight checked, attendees could find information on eye and foot problems, mental and dental health, arthritis, lung diseases, hearing aids, cancer screening, and diabetes. Many social agencies had booths to explain the availability of services for the elderly in the community.

Nine different films dealing with problems of the aging were shown. Student nurses from nearby universities assisted with the Fair.

Lakeside Elder Adult Project, Crescent Avenue United Methodist Church, 1232 Crescent Avenue, Fort Wayne, Indiana 46805.

§

Hearing Aid Bank

The Hearing Aid Bank of Ontario, California was established to benefit those with impaired hearing but whose financial situation would not permit the purchase of a new aid. Cosponsors are the First Baptist Church of Ontario and the Pomona Valley Council of Churches.

The Hearing Aid Bank is open from 10:00 A.M. until noon each Wednesday in the parish house of the First Baptist Church. On the third Wednesday of each month, testing equipment is brought in and hearing evaluations are made by a representative of the Valley Hearing Aid Center of Ontario. Eligibility for screening service is determined by income level and need. A person is encouraged to pay whatever amount he or she is able.

Hearing aids and funds are solicited through churches and community organizations. Although the First Baptist Church is providing office and testing space along with secretarial services free of charge, there are expenses involved in operating the program, repairing and adapting hearing aids for reuse, and purchasing new aids when a type needed is not available in the bank.

Hearing Aid Bank, First Baptist Church, 1305 North Euclid Avenue, Ontario, California 91762. The Reverend Ralph H. Lightbody, Pastor. (25¢)

Matthew 25 Health Clinic

This health clinic in Fort Wayne, Indiana is a voluntary organization operating strictly on donations from churches, industries, foundations, and individuals. Approximately 90% of the funds received go directly for patient care. The rest is for utilities, replenishment of medical supplies, and minimal upkeep on the building.

The Matthew 25 Health Clinic, which opened in a residence on May 1, 1976, is a free neighborhood clinic offering health screening, education, and referral services to those unable to pay for medical care. The need for such a service was first recognized by the pastor of St. Mary's Catholic Church, who found a group studying nonviolence willing to undertake the effort.

Doors of the Clinic are open to everyone regardless of race, religion, sex, or age. In the first 21 months of operation more than 1,500 patients were seen, more than a third of whom returned for at least one other visit. In addition to screening for particular problems, physicals were conducted for jobs, schools, sports, and general reasons. Pap smears and sickle cell tests were among the special examinations available free. Limited treatment is offered through prescriptions.

If a patient is in need of followup or of being under the care of a physician, they are helped through the Clinic's referral service. Several doctors and dentists have served referrals without charge to either the Matthew 25 Health Clinic or the patients. At least two hospitals have provided free lab work, and one has offered X-rays and filled prescriptions free of charge when patients were unable to pay. Doctor and dental bills, prescription costs, laboratory fees, etc., are paid by the Matthew 25 Health Clinic when necessary.

Doctors, nurses, and lab technicians working at the Clinic volunteer at least three hours a month. Other volunteers help with clerical work, transportation of patients, obtaining funds, and even with cleaning the building.

This Clinic is dedicated to making a reality the philosophy and justice expressed in Matthew 25:35-41: " . . . for I was hungry and you gave me food; I was thirsty and you gave me drink; I was a stranger and you welcomed me; I was naked and you clothed me; *I was sick and you cared for me;* I was in prison and you visited me" (italics ours).

Matthew 25 Health Clinic, 1117 Clay Street, Fort Wayne, Indiana 46802. Contact persons: Ted or Lynn Kurek, June Moord.

§

Housing Programs

1. Housing Action Alliance—Tenth Street Project
2. Jubilee Housing
3. Housing Opportunity Association
4. Connecticut Interfaith Housing
5. Housing for Senior Citizens and Families
6. Strawbridge Square
7. Community Renewal of Germantown

§

Housing Action Alliance—Tenth Street Project

Out of concern for disinvestment of capital, insurance, and public services in the inner-city area of Des Moines, Iowa, a coalition of religious organizations and their representatives (most functioning from a judicatory base of support) formed to agitate for reinstatement of such investment, and specifically to conduct a summer 1978 demonstration project in the rehabilitation of an inner-city block. The coalition, choosing the name Housing Action Alliance, was formed from vastly differing religious sectors: Southern Baptist, Catholic, United Methodist, United Presbyterian, Episcopalian, Lutheran, and Jewish.

A one-block stretch of Tenth Street between Enos and University was chosen for demonstrative action on the basis of at least 60% owner occupancy, resident interest, and need. Ten houses were involved, plus a small business.

The participating religious groups contributed seed money of $18,000 which, in turn, was used to seek matching funds from the Des Moines Housing Council, a group organized through the efforts of the chamber of commerce. The Council has a commitment to reverse disinvestment trends in the inner city, largely due to the agitation of such groups as the Housing Action Alliance. Eventually, the Housing Council is to obtain matching support from the city of Des Moines through revenue-sharing Neighborhood Development funds. Residents of the Tenth Street block have also contributed according to ability.

The major factor in the low-cost success of the project was a volunteer labor force: (1) 12 Jewish high-school-age youth from the New York City area under a special American Jewish Social Service project; (2) two VISTA workers who did mostly community cultivation and development and organizational work; and (3) a local youth work force under a summer youth employment program.

By September 1, 1978, the following had been accomplished:

- —Eight of the ten houses had been totally renovated, interior and exterior.
- —One house had been similarly renovated by the owner at his own expense (a resident employed by the Alliance to administer the project).
- —One house was slated for demolition and clearance.
- —A vacant lot piled high with rubbish was completely cleared.
- —A bootlegging operation in one of the houses was removed with the cooperation of residents and local authorities.
- —Signs of interest in home improvements became evident in the adjoining neighborhood.
- —A nearby neighborhood has taken enough hope for its preservation to resist a move by the city to change zoning from one- and two-family residential to multi-family.

The total cost for this phase of the work was $22,000 with another $5,000 available for Phase II, the winterizing and insulating of all homes in the block.

The Housing Action Alliance has tentatively decided to: (1) continue in a brokerage role to bring various persons and groups together for redevelopment action in the inner city; (2) serve a "goosage" function, mandating performance by agencies that should be acting for the well-being of the community; and (3) plan and carry out further rehabilitation projects. The Alliance stands by a firm commitment to assure the possibility of all residents of the inner city ("Model Cities" area) remaining in their neighborhoods if they choose.

Housing Action Alliance, 921 Pleasant, Des Moines, Iowa 50309. Kenneth Fineran, Urban Minister.

Jubilee Housing

Jubilee Housing, Inc., is a ministry of the Church of the Saviour in Washington, D.C. It was organized in 1973 by a group of concerned individuals already working actively in the inner city who saw a great need to improve the housing conditions of low-income people living in the city. Three objectives were established at the outset:

—to demonstrate that acceptable inner-city housing can be made available at costs within the budgets of low-income families;
—to encourage and sustain the participation of tenants in the operation and management of such housing; and
—to develop a model process from this experience which can be applied to other neighborhoods.

Jubilee Housing decided to focus energies on keeping low-rent apartment houses in the Adams-Morgan area, a section in which the poor were being displaced by the affluent. Two apartment buildings, the Ritz and the Mozart, were acquired along with a rehabilitation loan that had a sale-leaseback agreement with option for Jubilee to purchase at any time for cost. The two buildings, housing 90 families, were badly deteriorated, but rehabilitation to acceptable standards was initiated immediately with the tenants still in place.

Groups of volunteers were organized to clean the interior and exterior areas of the buildings and to remove trash. Apartments were upgraded one at a time to lessen dislocation of tenants. Elevators were restored to working order. Unless special skills or equipment were called for, the work was done by volunteers using donated or below-cost materials when available. More than 50,000 hours of volunteer work went into the restoration of these two buildings.

Other Jubilee volunteers worked with the residents in the development of social support programs. Children's programs were among the first to be established and ranged from summer day camps to winter swimming and tutoring sessions. A thrift store and a holistic health clinic were opened. A Montessori preschool and a community-based arts program were established. Programs have been changed or modified to meet the needs and interests of tenants.

As tenant leadership emerged, management cooperatives were developed. Responsibility for building operation and management now rests with resident boards of managers, supported by Jubilee volunteers.

In 1978, Jubilee Housing acquired the 32-unit Sorrento apartments on a neighboring corner. Here, resident management was developed from the beginning.

Jubilee Housing has a brochure and other publications that will be of interest to churches and groups wishing to undertake similar projects. ($1.00)

Jubilee Housing, Inc., 1750 Columbia Road, N.W., Washington, D.C. 20009.

§

Housing Opportunity Association

The Housing Opportunity Association of Lehigh Valley, Pennsylvania was organized in 1968 to assist families having difficulty in finding adequate housing. Most were unable to qualify for either public housing or private mortgages. (See page 54 of text.)

After determining the needs of an applicant, the Housing Opportunity Association finds a house, secures a mortgage from a local bank, makes renovations, and then enters into a rental or purchase agreement. A family wishing to buy is asked to raise $500 toward the down payment. H.O.A.'s investment is regarded as a loan, which the family repays in monthly installments that include mortgage and interest. On repayment of the loan, H.O.A. transfers title and mortgage, thus letting the family assume the responsibility of home ownership.

The directors of the Housing Opportunity Association maintain a close relationship with all the families being served, providing guidance in such areas as employment, health, and consumer protection.

The present board has decided to limit to 25 the number of families that can be helped at any one time in order to continue as a volunteer organization. All funds go directly into housing. However, the directors will be glad to assist in establishing similar programs in the Bethlehem area.

The Housing Opportunity Association, supported at first through contributions from churches and individuals, has developed a revolving fund to carry on its work.

Housing Opportunity Association, c/o Mrs. Voris V. Latshaw, 275 Buckingham Drive, Bethlehem, Pennsylvania 18017. (25¢)

§

Connecticut Interfaith Housing

An ecumenical effort to generate housing for low- and moderate-income families and the elderly, and to protect nonprofit sponsors from loss, began in 1968 with the formation of the Connecticut Interfaith Housing Corporation. Incorporators included the Archdiocese of Hartford, Episcopal Diocese of Connecticut, Diocese of Norwich, United Church of Christ (Connecticut Conference), and the United Methodist Church (New York and Western Connecticut Conference). Each judicatory made two commitments: to provide housing technicians on a part-time basis and to make an annual contribution to C.I.H. for its operations. Later on, each group contributed a one-time $25,000 to a revolving loan fund.

In the first ten years over 1,600 units were constructed by Connecticut churches with assistance from C.I.H. In several projects, support social services were pledged for the length of the mortgage.

One of the successful C.I.H. related projects is the Davenport Residence in Hamden. A 217-suite highrise sheltered by tall pines, it is within easy walking distance of shops, churches, a movie theater, and the post office, and only a short bus ride away from New Haven. Designed for healthy people with moderate means, Davenport reserves the 55 one-bedroom apartments for couples. The United Church of Christ has provided a social program that won for Davenport Residence a 1976 award from the Department of Housing and Urban Development.

In Norwalk, St. Paul's Housing—a Section 236 development for 86 families—opened in December 1974. This project was undertaken after St. Paul's Church determined housing to be the most pressing need of the community. The committee processing the first applications (600 of them!) tried to maintain a balance in selecting 41 black, 15 Spanish-speaking and 30 "other" families. Though drained by the experience, they immediately offered help to others looking for direction in sponsoring a similar development.

Washington Heights apartments offer independent living to elderly and physically handicapped persons over 18. Almost as soon as the 120-unit building was opened, plans were moving ahead for a second building. The First Baptist Church of Bridgeport sponsored the project and it is managed by the American Baptist Corporation. Tenants are particularly appreciative of emergency call buttons connecting the units with the manager's office and apartment.

These three projects provided only 513 of the 1,600 units completed by 1978. A status report at the end of 1978 shows 22 communities constructing or planning hundreds of additional units with the help of Connecticut Interfaith Housing.

With the encouragement of the United Church of Christ, the New England Non-Profit Housing Development Corporation has published *A Guide to the Design and Development of Housing for the Elderly.* Copies of this 90-page book are available from the New England Non-Profit Housing Development Corporation, 28 South Main Street, Concord, New Hampshire 03301, and from Helen Webber, Board of Homeland Ministries, United Church of Christ, 297 Park Avenue South, New York, New York 10010.

Connecticut Interfaith Housing Corporation, 99 Jackson Street, Willimantic, Connecticut 06226.

§

Housing for Senior Citizens and Families

Inter/Serv (Interfaith Community Services) of St. Joseph, Missouri has entered into housing for both senior citizens and for low- and moderate-income families.

Wesley Senior Towers, a 12-story high-rise apartment complex in downtown St. Joesph, was opened in 1977 with 121 persons occupying the 110 units—and 500 names on the waiting list. This is fulfilling a great need for senior citizens who did not wish to leave the inner city but wanted a sense of security and companionship. Every service of the city, including a park and churches, is within easy walking distance.

A year later the *St. Francis Apartments,* with 72 units in a three-story building and 35 in four-plex units, opened for senior citizens in a suburban area of the city. Six of the apartments have two bedrooms; all others, one. Ten percent of the units are equipped for the handicapped, and all have a patio or balcony.

The *Northwood Apartments* were built to accommodate families displaced by highway construction. This is a suburban complex for moderate-income families needing one and two bedrooms. The *Oakridge Apartments* were developed to care for large families in the inner city who were unable to find adequate housing. Most of the Oakridge units have three or four bedrooms, and minority families occupy at least half of the apartments. Inter/Serv provides a variety of social services.

In all four housing developments, utilities are furnished. Rent is based on 25% of a tenant's income.

Interfaith Community Services, 200 Cherokee Street, St. Joseph, Missouri 64504. Don McCreary, Coordinator for Housing.

Strawbridge Square

A 128 subsidized rental townhouse and garden apartment development providing one-, two-, three-, and four-bedroom units was opened for occupancy in the Lincolnia section of Fairfax County, Virginia in September 1979.

Called Strawbridge Square, it exists because 99 United Methodist churches felt the need to help increase the supply of decent housing for persons of low and moderate incomes. The churches formed a nonprofit corporation known as the Wesley Housing Development Corporation of Northern Virginia. The 20-acre site was donated. The National Corporation of Housing Partnerships, as general partner, has provided the needed capital for development.

Six one-bedroom townhouses are designed to accommodate wheel chairs. All townhouse units have private patios and face pedestrian spaces with pathways, benches, and public garden areas. Both townhouses and apartments are centrally air conditioned. Larger units have laundry hookups, and a central laundry facility is located in the management complex.

Recreational facilities include three playgrounds for small children, basketball courts, lounge areas, and a multipurpose room. The county plans to build a community center. An eight-acre park with nature trails is located near the development.

The Department of Housing and Urban Development has determined the economic mix: 70% of the tenants will be of moderate income, 30% will be of low income, and a maximum of 10% will be welfare recipients. H.U.D. criteria also identify low and moderate incomes.

Any person or family qualified to live in Strawbridge Square will spend only 25% of their gross income for rent. Utilities are included in this amount. The balance of the rent will be paid through an H.U.D. Section appropriation. (Fair market rents are set by H.U.D. for each unit.)

The project will be managed by the National Corporation for Housing Management. In addition, Strawbridge Square, Inc., a wholly owned subsidiary of the Wesley Housing Development Corporation, will oversee management by N.C.H.M. to double insure that quality and caring management takes place. Strawbridge Square, Inc., which has two residents from the adjacent community on its board of directors, has the authority to demand a new managing agent in the event it is felt one is needed.

Wesley Housing Development Corporation, 4701 Arlington Boulevard, Arlington, Virginia 22203. Virginia Peters, Executive Director.

Community Renewal of Germantown

When proposals were made to upgrade the commercial section of Germantown Avenue, members of the First United Methodist Church of Germantown asked what would happen to the residents living there. On a quick walk of the area, they discovered that there were ten abandoned homes in the block immediately adjacent to the church.

A dozen church members began working on means of acquiring and rehabilitating these abandoned houses. Concurrently, they formed a corporation under the name of Community Renewal of Germantown with representation equally divided between church members and community residents.

The first house was renovated at a cost of $11,000 and thousands of weekend hours of volunteer labor, including that of local school groups. The $5,000 profit realized from the sale of the house will pay for interest on loans and for materials toward renovation of the next house.

It took four years to reach this first goal. During that period there have been numerous celebrations, bringing the church and community closer together. Best of all, the spirit has caught on in the neighborhood and other public and private groups have begun renovation on some of the other abandoned homes.

First United Methodist Church of Germantown, 6023 Germantown Avenue, Philadelphia, Pennsylvania 19144. Mrs. Rosemary Walkenhorst, Chairperson.

§

Hunger Programs

1. St. Mary's Food Bank
2. Doof Foods, Co-op
3. Walk for the Hungry
4. Fast for World Hunger
5. Gleaners Statewide
6. Care & Share
7. The Garden Patch
8. The Food Bank

§

St. Mary's Food Bank

The St. Mary's Food Bank of Phoenix, Arizona, in operation since 1967, now has three basic thrusts: the Food Bank Salvage Program, the Food Box Program, and Second Harvest. (See page 59 for background information.)

The *St. Mary's Food Bank Salvage Program* continues to be a clearinghouse of surplus and salvaged food for over 250 local agencies, churches, charities, AA houses, Indian schools, and nursing homes. All recipients must be nonprofit organizations who do "on premises feeding" and will promise to use the donated food immediately. They also sign disclaimers freeing both St. Mary's and the original donors of the food from responsibility.

Some of the salvageable food products are: day-old bakery goods, dented canned goods, broken packaging, shrinkage ice cream, bruised meat products, mistakes in manufacturing and labeling, produce too small or too large for package sizes, etc. More than two million pounds of salvage food was distributed at St. Mary's in 1978.

The Food Bank has been staffed through the years with volunteers with some assistance from the CETA program. Without salaries to pay, St. Mary's Food Bank Salvage Program has been able to operate with a very low budget, all of which has been met through contributions.

St. Mary's Food Bank Food Box Program was established in 1969 to help solve emergency food needs of Phoenix families. (Arizona does not have an emergency food stamp program.) Boxes provide enough food for a family of four for three days and are given only to those families who are seeking longer-term help through community and social workers. A family is limited to three emergency food boxes in a six-month period.

All items in a food box are in perfect condition. About 95% of the canned goods comes in through drives conducted by churches, Scout groups, and other civic organizations. In addition, $800 is spent each week for groceries to insure that nutritionally balanced meals can be prepared from the food boxes.

The Food Box Program is also staffed by volunteers. All contributions go to purchase food. The building used has been provided by the city of Phoenix for a fee of one dollar a year.

Second Harvest was born in 1975 when the Community Services Administration gave the St. Mary's Food Bank a grant to help other communities establish food banks. In its first three years, Second Harvest has provided training and technical assistance to hundreds of people, organizations, and coalitions interested in alleviating hunger. Second Harvest has been instrumental in the organization of 30 food bank salvage programs and 50 or more food box programs.

A newsletter, "Thought For Food," is one avenue Second Harvest is using for the sharing of experiences and information among the food banks in this growing network.

While conducting hunger workshops across the country, Second Harvest leaders have been contacting officials in the food industry. Corporations are expressing a willingness to donate truckloads of surplus food, in exchange for the tax benefits, provided deliveries can be made to the nearest food bank. Thus, Second Harvest sees itself becoming the national clearinghouse for the sharing of food among food banks over the country, just as St. Mary's became the clearinghouse for food shared by many local agencies.

St. Mary's Food Bank, 819 North Third Street, Phoenix, Arizona 85004. John Van Hengel, Director.

Doof Foods, Co-op

This food-buying club in Albuquerque, New Mexico was started in 1976 with three goals: (1) to put into practice a concern about hunger and nutrition; (2) to bring together people of all ages in a common project; and (3) to address the need for alternative, non-agribusiness-controlled food sources. Doof Foods is typical of many cooperatives in requiring a small membership fee (to cover overhead expenses) and a sharing in the work. Food is sold at cost. Distribution is made monthly from the University Heights United Methodist Church, which supports the project.

Members have successfully related to the three original concerns. The availability of whole grains, flours, pastas, legumes and cheese at reasonable prices has influenced many people to improve their eating habits. Doof Foods has brought together people of various faiths and social classes as well as all ages. Members have been active in lobbying congresspersons to support legislation that would permit food-stamp recipients to participate in buying clubs and to vote for the Co-op Bank Bill.

At least one other co-op has been organized as a result of Doof Food's mission outreach, and several other churches and groups have expressed interest.

University Heights United Methodist Church, 2210 Silver, S.E., Albuquerque, New Mexico 87106. Contact Person, Don Hancock. (25¢)

(Editor's note: Members of a similar co-op held monthly covered-dish suppers for the sharing of buying and nutritional information and for compiling the monthly order.)

§

Walk for the Hungry

Most churches and communities are familiar with "walks" for world hunger. Children and youth volunteer to walk a specified route on a particular day. Each participant solicits sponsors willing to pledge so much for each mile walked.

To be successful, a "walk" for the hungry needs to be carefully planned, coordinated, and supervised. Pledges need to be collected promptly.

CROP, the Community Hunger Appeal of Church World Service, stands ready to help. Pledge cards, collection envelopes, and organizational materials are yours for the asking.

All funds from a CROP Walk for the Hungry are used by Church World

Service, the agency through which some 30 denominations bring relief and development aid to people in great need. Hunger is alleviated through eight program categories on five continents and in over 50 countries, including our own.

Other CROP hunger programs to bring in funds include: fasts, canvasses, vacation church school projects, and marathons of all types. Films and filmstrips are available to stimulate interest.

National CROP Office, Elkhart, Indiana 46515. Or, write to the CROP Regional Office nearest you.

§

Fast for World Hunger

Trinity United Methodist Church in Racine, Wisconsin had a church-wide emphasis on world hunger in November, 1978. Adults participated in a two-day seminar early in the month, and special programs on hunger were presented to the youth and children.

To increase awareness of what it means to be hungry, it was decided to have a 30-hour fast (only water permitted) from 8:00 A.M. on Saturday, November 18, until the following day at 2:00 P.M. Each participant was encouraged to give the amount saved on meals for world hunger.

In addition, friends of the fasters were asked to serve as sponsors by pledging an amount for each hour a certain person fasted. Pledges could also be made for any portion of someone's fast—such as the last five hours. Sign-up sheets were available to participants for getting the names and pledges of sponsors.

Many fasters were participating in an intentional fast for the first time. Afterwards they agreed that they would be much more sensitive to the plight of the world's poor in the future. They voiced special concern for the women and children who are victims of circumstances they cannot control. The monies collected were forwarded to the Missional Priority on World Hunger of the United Methodist Church.

Trinity United Methodist Church, 3825 Erie Street, Racine, Wisconsin 53403. The Reverend William Carlson, Pastor.

§

Gleaners Statewide

Gleaners Statewide is a self-help charity in California that salvages food that would otherwise go to waste. In return for their labor, workers keep what they can use and distribute the balance to low-income senior citizens through other charities.

Members are retirees who volunteer to glean fields after the regular harvest. They travel a radius of 50 miles at their own expense and, in addition, pay an annual fee of $14 per family to cover the costs of locating farmers willing to let them glean fields, trees, and vines.

A great variety of produce is picked: pears, peaches, tomatoes, watermelons, sweet potatoes, onions, Irish potatoes, cauliflower, cabbages, artichokes, lettuce, persimmons, figs, grapes, cherries, apricots, and much more. Hundreds of tons of food are salvaged each year.

Many organizations support the efforts of Gleaners Statewide. Business persons have provided free truck rentals, office equipment, typewriter repairs, etc. A church has donated rent-free a building for storage.

Gleaners Statewide is headquartered in Sacramento and has chapters in the four adjacent counties. Plans call for continued expansion until the organization is statewide in fact as well as in name.

Gleaners Statewide, c/o Homer Fahrner, 2606½ J Street, Box D, Sacramento, California 95816. (50¢)

§

Care & Share

The food-buying cooperative of Grace United Methodist Church in Minneapolis, Minnesota could well serve as a model for other churches. (See page 95.)

Care & Share is a biweekly operation for the buying of fresh produce, cheese, and eggs. Many nonperishable items can be ordered at six-week intervals. It should be noted that provisions have been made to include shut-ins in the cooperative, with volunteers making the deliveries.

Bills for each order show the difference between the actual cost of the items and the comparable cost at retail. Those participants who can contribute this difference to the Care & Share Fund, from which thousands of dollars have gone out to relieve the hunger and sufferings of others. Through it, Grace Church has helped two Vietnamese families to get established in Minneapolis, the most recent family in 1979.

Care & Share, Grace United Methodist Church, 2510 N. E. Cleveland, Minneapolis, Minnesota 55418. The Reverend James H. Schneider, Minister.

The Garden Patch

The Church of the Brethren, Root River in Preston, Minnesota sells excess garden produce for half the current market value at the Garden Patch, a booth open half a day each week during the growing season. Vegetables and fruits are gathered from local community gardens. The booth is near to, and the gift of, a supermarket that also usually buys what is left at the end of the day. Any excess is donated to a hospital/nursing home and a halfway home for retarded adults. Income from the Garden Patch is contributed to local, national, and international hunger and service programs.

The Patch is an outgrowth of a continuing study in the church of world hunger and provides an opportunity for sharing hunger and nutritional information with others. Although anyone may shop at the Garden Patch, senior citizens on fixed and limited incomes have found it a way to enrich their diets with homegrown foods at prices they can afford.

Church of the Brethren, Root River, Route 2, Preston, Minnesota 55965. James E. Tomlonson, Pastor. (25¢)

§

The Food Bank

The Tri-County Community Council of Portland, Oregon discovered in 1975 that not all hungry people live in faraway places. In their own tri-county region, 100,000 people were living below poverty level. And yet, while many of these were hungry, food was going to waste in fields, stores, food plants, and restaurants.

The Food Bank, a nonprofit organization, in the first couple years of operation salvaged over 950,000 pounds of edible food—food that would otherwise have been discarded. Oregon farmers, who receive a tax credit for contributions, were encouraged to open their fields to volunteer gleaners. Dated, damaged, and surplus foodstuffs were solicited from the food industry. These contributors are eligible for a tax deduction of up to half the retail value of the donated goods.

The Food Bank is willing to pick up food and to deliver it to the 23 member social agencies. Approximately 50 other nonprofit groups have received food from the bank on occasion.

Speakers and a slide show are available to explain area hunger problems to civic, church, and school groups.

The Food Bank, 718 West Burnside, Portland, Oregon 97209.

Multiservice Programs

1. Crosslines
2. Inter-Church Council for Social Service
3. Churchpeople for Change and Reconciliation
4. Human Needs Appeal
5. FISH Volunteer Program
6. The Good Samaritan Association
7. Block Partnership
8. Capitol Hill Group Ministry
9. The Solid Rock
10. Tacoma Community House

§

Crosslines

Crosslines is a volunteer organization using members from more than 30 churches in Springfield, Missouri to meet human needs with Christian compassion. There is no paid staff.

Crosslines maintains a telephone answering service to match needs with sources of help. Volunteers provide transportation, food, medical care, legal counsel, marriage counseling, tutoring, and babysitting for persons unable to arrange for these services for themselves. Crosslines also has a temporary shelter program, a furniture distribution center, and a clothing bank. The Crosslines Distribution Center is open Monday through Friday from 9:00 A.M. to 3:00 P.M.

The participating churches, referred to as "Fish Churches," collect food, clothing, household items, and furniture, and supply the volunteers needed to operate the program one day a month. Financial contributions are used to defray the costs of operating the distribution center and for the temporary family shelter program.

Crosslines, Box 3686, Glenstone Station, Springfield, Missouri 65804. Mrs. Betty Schlesing, Volunteer Director.

Inter-Church Council for Social Service

Nearly 200 volunteers working with three staff consultants carry on a broad program of social service and action through the Inter-Church Council for Social Service in Chapel Hill, North Carolina.

The Family Assistance Program alleviates problems of housing, food, and health through direct services and referrals to other agencies. Emergency financial needs are often met with small interest-free loans from I.C.C.'s Loan and Grant Fund. A person needing help to become self-sustaining can borrow from the Individual Development Fund for such items as technical training, required uniforms for a new job, and job-related equipment.

As an outgrowth of coordinating services provided by church volunteers to nursing homes, the Inter-Church Council organized an advocacy group, Friends of Nursing Home Patients. The new group now has its own staff and funding.

A concern for alcoholics led to the establishing of a detoxification center. Though the center is now operated independently of I.C.C., volunteers are still committed to increasing services for alcoholics. There is also a program to help ex-offenders find jobs and adjust to society when released from prison.

Neighbors Reaching In is a project to locate and assist neighbors to help each other with social problems, especially among the elderly.

Past achievements of the Inter-Church Council for Social Service include:

- —Built 79 units of low- and moderate-income housing.
- —Operated the first integrated summer day camp in the Chapel Hill-Carrboro area.
- —Started preschool tutoring program before Headstart.
- —Operated a free legal aid service on three different occasions when government funding was not available.

The Inter-Church Council maintains an information and referral service. Its most recent efforts have gone into setting up a Health Consumer Organization and trying to find funding for moderate-cost housing for the elderly.

Financial support comes from more than 20 churches, the United Fund, individuals, and community organizations. Volunteer workers are from the churches and community.

Inter-Church Council for Social Service, 207 Wilson Street, Chapel Hill, North Carolina 27514. Contact person: Dorothy Mullen.

Churchpeople for Change and Reconciliation

Nine major Christian denominations in Lima and Allen County, Ohio have joined hands in an impressive ecumenical ministry. Through Churchpeople for Change and Reconciliation, they attempt to bring the Christian gospel to bear on local social problems.

C.C.R. policies, goals, and priorities are determined by an executive board of 18 (two from each denomination). There are two full-time staff persons, a director-coordinator, and a secretary. Program activities are organized through committees composed of local church people. Funding comes from the nine sponsoring denominations, and office space is provided by one of the cooperating churches.

Through its many outreach programs, Churchpeople for Change and Reconciliation:

—provides a jail ministry that includes a chaplaincy program, arts and crafts for women inmates, a court watching project, and the Allen County Corrections Concern Association.

—monitors City Council meetings and urges members to effect legislation that will benefit the poor, the elderly, and minorities.

—uses TV and radio to prick the consciences of people and to motivate them to apply their religion to societal problems.

—cooperates with the Allen Metropolitan Housing Authority in providing decent and adequate housing for the elderly.

—encourages low-income families, through the REHAB project, to become home owners. REHAB, a program initiated by Churchpeople for Change and Reconciliation, offers extensive assistance in restoring neglected houses, in helping low-income families to buy a restored house on the open market, and in helping families improve home maintenance and management skills. REHAB believes that the poverty cycle can best be broken by directly involving individuals in a self-development process designed to help them help themselves.

—plans to rebuild and revitalize deteriorating neighborhoods. Redevelopment of both residential and commercial properties in Kibby Corners is already well underway. Residents and business persons are working with both Churchpeople for Change and Reconciliation and government agencies to provide buildings and community services.

Churchpeople for Change and Reconciliation, 221 West North Street, Lima, Ohio 45801. The Reverend Leonard A. Stark, Director.

§

Human Needs Appeal

The University United Methodist Temple of Seattle, Washington annually raises approximately $8,000 in a Human Needs Appeal to be disbursed on a percentage basis for existing programs in the community. Selection of the agencies to be helped is made by the Commission on Social Concerns. Members of the congregation are given a list of the organizations with their addresses and brief program descriptions. The 1977-78 Appeal enabled University Temple to assist:

- —a Methodist-affiliated center working with single adolescent parents, potential or actual delinquents, and other youth needing social services;
- —a center organized by and for the people of the inner city offering hospitality, counseling, health care, and "Operation Night Watch";
- —a United Methodist home for children with problems best dealt with in a residential setting;
- —a clinic utilizing the services of over 200 volunteers and 10 full-time staff persons in providing 24-hour medical and social services;
- —a nonprofit corporation providing inexpensive transportation and housing for inmates of the Walla Walla State Prison from the Seattle area who wish to visit families and friends;
- —a draft counseling office working with 18-year-olds and youth already in the military who have questions of conscience;
- —an interchurch project providing a program of day services for disabled older adults;
- —a project to start a shelter for physically and emotionally abused women and their children;
- —a fund used for the special emergency needs of Indians in the Greater Seattle area;
- —a training program to upgrade the skills and competence of black pastors in leadership roles, and to provide avenues to help them deal with such community problems as housing, criminal justice, problems of the aged, etc.;
- —a discretionary fund to be held in reserve and dispersed through the year as special human needs arise.

University United Methodist Temple, c/o Robert Shaw, 512 Wellington Avenue, Seattle 98122.

§

Fish Volunteer Program

FISH volunteer programs in the United States, using a similar effort in England as a model, supply on an anonymous basis emergency services for persons not able to provide for themselves, or for whom no other provision is made within the community.

The FISH program in Des Moines, Iowa began as a ministry of one local church. Soon calls for assistance were coming in from the entire city, highlighting a need for services and also the need for more volunteers.

The program is now a department of the Des Moines Area Religious Council, and volunteers from 35 different congregations, representing 11 denominations, are participating in it. Calls for help are received by an answering service and relayed to the volunteer who is coordinating the program for that 24-hour period. This person, in turn, selects from the dozens of volunteers on the stand-by list and calls the one best able to meet the immediate need. It may be a request for emergency transportation to a hospital or doctor, babysitting for a family where someone has suddenly been hospitalized, reading to the blind, etc.

The Des Moines FISH program averages about 165 calls a month and is able to respond by direct services or making referrals to other agencies to about 80-85% of all requests for help. The program is supported in terms of direct cost by special contributions.

Des Moines Area Religious Council, 3829 Grand Avenue, Des Moines, Iowa 50312. The Reverend Harold Varce, contact person.

§

The Good Samaritan Association

The seeds for the Good Samaritan Association, well known in the San Diego area for meeting the calls of the poor, lonely, and despairing, were sown by two persons when they delivered their first emergency food box and then continued to respond to other needs in the community. That was back in 1971. Three years later their efforts became the outreach program of a local parish, and by 1977 the Good Samaritan Association incorporated as an independent nonprofit organization dedicated to fulfilling the parable of the Good Samaritan (Luke 10:33-35).

All Samaritan members volunteer their services, eliminating operating expenses except for such miscellaneous items as printing and postage. The talents volunteered have included those of an artist and illustrator, writer and editor, nurse and theologian, bookkeeper and chef, priest and lawyer, secretary and homemaker.

The Good Samaritans seek out and serve people in need regardless of age or race. However, more and more time and effort is going into creatively solving the problems and needs of the elderly in their 80s and 90s who are partially or totally homebound. Volunteers ask only those questions that enable them to know the needs and to respond to them.

Though services may fall under the general categories of financial assistance, food, clothing, medicine, a kind word, or an hour's time, a more detailed report might show the following: an apartment cleaned for a disabled senior citizen, a TV set (the only source of entertainment) sent out for repair at the Association's expense, safety guards installed so that an arthritic person can continue to live independently, a "slush fund" set up for a terminally ill patient, a delinquent utility bill paid to prevent termination of service, or a bedridden patient given a shave, haircut, or shampoo.

Emergency food boxes of prepackaged, nonperishable items are delivered on the same day the requests are received. "Angel Food Kits" of easily prepared but highly nutritional items are offered to persons living alone who are suddenly homebound or in an emergency situation.

Each year a Christmas dinner is served to the physically and mentally disabled living in nearby centers and hospitals, to long-term patients living in convalescent hospitals and rest homes, and to the needy and lonely in the community. Guests receive gifts as well as dinner and are provided transportation. Needy community families are given food baskets for celebrations within their own homes. These holiday efforts are made possible through the one big fund-raising event of the year, "An Evening of Roses," held in September.

In addition to the "Evening of Roses," the work of the Good Samaritans is supported through contributions and memberships. No federal funding has been or will be accepted.

As a result of their experiences through the years, the Samaritans are committed to the following: "It is in the Process of Declared Christian Volunteerism that the opposites—the volunteer and the recipient—are brought together, uncovering a spirit of truth, honesty, and respect in one another. In this union of honest caring, giving and receiving, the Good Samaritans hope to bring about a Christian Presence in all humankind."

(See page 56 in text for additional information.)

The Good Samaritan Association, P.O. Box 7812, San Diego, California 92107. Rose T. Ebner, Director.

Block Partnership

The Greater Dallas Community of Churches organizes people in deprived areas around their community problems and then matches them with nonresident partners in its Block Partnership program. Thus, this people-to-people program strives to involve residents in determining their own destiny while sensitizing the nonresident partners to the real needs of the inner city.

Inner city residents are brought together by a staff organizer who works through existing structures when possible. After the group is meeting on a regular basis, residents are asked if they would like to work through the Block Partnership. If so, boundaries are set, priorities established, and a membership application submitted.

Nonresident groups, usually churches, willing to work in a poor section, are sought and screened. In some cases, two churches will choose to work together. Nonresident groups also submit membership applications.

Prospective Block Partners are brought together before the Partnership Agreement is signed. Sometimes expectations on both sides, unless known in advance, could prevent the partnership from being effective.

The Partners work together for a specified length of time, usually six months. Anything from a low-income home ownership program to a day-care center can be started. The nonresident group may need to raise funds, find doctors and lawyers willing to donate their professional services, etc.

The Greater Dallas Community of Churches has two other similar programs. In one, the School Partnership, churches and groups are matched with schools within the Dallas Independent School District to provide support to enrich the education of every child. In the other, the House Partnership program, the skills and resources of churches and groups are matched to the needs of indigent home-owners. Houses are brought up to acceptable city standards and the quality of life improved.

Block Partnership, 2801 Peabody at Oakland, Dallas, Texas 75215. For School and House Partnership information, write to the *Greater Dallas Community of Churches,* 901 Ross Avenue, Dallas, Texas 75202.

§

Capitol Hill Group Ministry

Since 1966, the Capitol Hill Group Ministry has been bringing the clergy and laity of 20 or more churches together for study, discussion, and action in addressing the socio-economic and psychological needs of the Capitol Hill area in Washington, D. C. The radical restoration of this section of the city has caused the displacement of thousands of persons—low- and moderate-income families along with many senior citizens living in homes owned by their families for several decades. However, low-income families remain in federally owned housing projects and in unrestored homes bordering the area.

The Capitol Hill Group Ministry provides three direct services:

—The *Teen Center,* open every evening from 7:00 to 10:00 P.M., offers a variety of recreational activities for the youth of the community. The Center successfully sponsored the Capitol Hill Invitation Basketball Tournament.

—*Free Tax Clinics* provide low-income individuals with assistance in filing local and federal income tax forms without fee. An attorney, who resides on Capitol Hill, directs the program, which recruits and trains volunteers as tax assistants.

—The *Emergency Food Program* is a cooperative effort of 30 churches and Friendship House, a community social agency, to feed the hungry. Food and cash are collected by the churches and taken regularly to the Emergency Food Bank, from which food is distributed as needed by the Consumer Action director of Friendship House. Referrals are made by the participating churches.

The Capitol Hill Group Ministry has become increasingly concerned about the senior citizens who can no longer afford to maintain their homes and apartments on the Hill. Efforts are being made to have the grounds of a former hospital, now owned by congress, designated for new housing for low- and moderate-income senior citizens. Churches of the area contributed the funds for a feasibility study, and C.H.G.M. is providing the leadership in seeking the conversion. Present plans call for 160 apartment units.

Capitol Hill Group Ministry, 327 North Carolina Avenue, S.E., Washington, D. C. 20003.

§

The Solid Rock

Reorganized in 1976, The Solid Rock is a non-profit, multiservice corporation which is interdenominational and ecumenical on all policy-making and operational levels.

The Solid Rock is based in the former Protestant Indian Student Center in Brigham City, Utah, built by the United Prebyterian Church adjacent to Intermountain Inter-Tribal High School. This federally supported Indian boarding school served only Navajo youth for 24 years but now has a student body representing more than 20 tribes and many states.

There continues to be a strong Protestant Indian Student Ministry at The Solid Rock. It is an "oasis" away from the campus for recreation, small study and discussion groups, worship and personal growth experiences, fellowship, and counseling.

Services have been expanded to include the New Life Youth Program for elementary school children of working and/or single parents. Once-a-week "clubs" are held for various age groups to help children develop self-esteem, confidence, and an appreciation of others. Gardening, cooking, and recreation are among the activities led by volunteers.

The Box Elder Community Pantry is a direct service program at The Solid Rock to provide emergency help to individuals and families living in Box Elder County and to transients in need. Community Pantry volunteers provide food, lodging, transportation, and clothing. Referrals are also made to social welfare agencies. Food, money, and volunteers for the Pantry come from local churches with additional funding from the Federal Community Action Program and United Way.

While new projects are being developed, The Solid Rock continues to offer its facilities for local church programs, a Day Care Center for Developmentally Disabled, an ecumenical publication center, a Catholic educational program, and a myriad of other activities. Summer Youth Work Camps are hosted to provide opportunities and experiences in Christian development and service for youth who are willing, in turn, to help with the maintenance and upkeep of The Solid Rock.

The Solid Rock, 435 East Seventh South, Brigham City, Utah 84302. Eldon H. Coffman, Director. ($1.00)

§

Tacoma Community House

Tacoma Community House has a history dating back to January 4, 1907, when the Home Missionary Board of the Methodist Church appointed a committee to organize missionary work in Tacoma. Three years later a house was rented and service to the neighborhood began. The first programs were primarily for children and youth, but the Community House has changed its programs through the years to meet the needs of the area.

In the 1930s, there was a need for direct relief work and the establishing of an employment bureau. This was the period when the Community House began opening its doors free of charge to other community organizations for meetings and recreation, a policy that still exists.

In the 50s and 60s, the Community House became multiracial out of necessity. It was serving every race, 23 different nationalities, and 22 denominations. With so many new neighbors, some of them immigrants, the Community House renewed its efforts to bring about better understanding among all neighborhood peoples.

The emphasis of programming was on families until the late 1960's when federal poverty programs duplicated much of what was being done. The Community House then moved to become an enabler, changing from providing services to providing an approach for the neighborhood to request its own services.

It was soon realized that the Asian Americans were a significant minority in the Tacoma-Pierce County area and that services to them as a community were practically nonexistent. By 1973, the major resources of the Community House were concentrated toward enablement and empowerment of the Asian community. This has continued to be a major focus to the present. Ongoing services to Indochinese refugees and other Asian immigrants include newsletters, crisis intervention, interpretation and translation, and English as a Second Language classes.

And as needs continue to change, the Community House has moved to establish a strong program of recreation with their gym facility open and in use seven days a week. Many outdoor activities are also a part of the recreation program.

Tacoma Community House, Post Office Box 5107, Tacoma, Washington 98405. The Reverend Robert Yamashita, Director.

§

Peace Programs

1. Infant Formula Action
2. Peace Projects
3. World Peacemakers
4. Trick or Treat for UNICEF
5. Foreign Student Weekend

§

Infant Formula Action

The effort to hold milk companies accountable for promotion of artificial feeding of babies in Third World countries is discussed in chapter seven (see page 91.)

Concern has grown steadily since the first reports linking increased malnutrition among infants in developing countries to the selling of powdered formula were published in the early 1970s. American companies have responded to pressures brought by shareholder resolutions, with churches playing a leading role in the effort. In July 1977, congress amended the International Development and Food Assistance Act to develop a "strategy for programs of nutrition and health improvements . . . including breastfeeding."

Today the focus is on Nestlé Company, a Swiss based corporation. A boycott of their products is one way of voicing concern over their continued promotion of infant formula in the Third World.

Boycott information, program resources, educational materials, and lists of available films can be secured from the following organizations:

INFACT (Infant Formula Action Coalition), 1701 University Avenue, S.E., Minneapolis, Minnesota 55414.

Interfaith Center on Corporate Responsibility, 475 Riverside Drive, Room 566, New York, New York 10115.

CALC (Clergy and Laity Concerned), 198 Broadway, New York, New York, 10038.

§

Peace Projects

Chapter seven suggests many ways in which a local church can work for peace. Rather than explore more models, this section will offer sources of help.

First, check to see if your own denomination has an office dealing with peace and justice issues. If there is one, write to find out what resources are available. Perhaps they will have names of speakers or workshop leaders in your area.

Another possible source for help is the Institute for World Order, an organization involved in promoting the values of peace, social justice, economic well-being, and ecological balance through research and education. The Institute has published as a public service a little pamphlet called "How to Work for Peace." Also available is "A Preliminary Directory of Organizations and Publications for Peace and World Order Educators," prepared by the Institute's Transnational Academic Program. The address is: *Institute for World Order,* 1140 Avenue of the Americas, New York, New York 10036.

Church groups wishing to explore the whole questions of investing in companies that are non-war-related might write to the *Interfaith Center on Corporate Responsibility,* 475 Riverside Drive, Room 566, New York, New York 10115. Films and other materials are available.

If you wish additional information on ways to observe Human Rights Day, write to the *United Nations Association of the U.S.A.,* 300 East 42nd Street, New York, New York 10017. Be sure to ask for a list of resource and gift items. Questions on the Human Rights Day celebrations in Washington, D.C., can be directed to Ms. Sophie Degan, Capital Area Division, U.N.A.-U.S.A., 3141 N Street, N.W., Washington, D.C. 20007.

World Peacemakers

World Peacemakers was organized by Gordon Cosby and Richard J. Barnet of the Church of the Saviour, Washington, D.C., who are personally committing themselves to work for and to enlist others in the cause of peace. (See page 86 of text.)

Two strategies have been developed thus far. The first is a letter-writing campaign by individuals to friends and relatives to raise the issue of the arms race and to encourage them to write similar letters. World Peacemakers has published a series of World Peace Papers and has a newsletter which can be used as enclosures.

The second strategy is the establishing of local Peacemaker Groups, sustained and directed by the inward journey of peacemaking (prayer disciplines, group worship, study, etc.), to journey outward in specific acts of peacemaking decided upon by the group. Gordon Cosby says: "As the group learns and grows together, and as the political scene changes, the strategies of the group will expand and fluctuate also." Out of one workshop held by World Peacemakers in November 1978, 15 Peacemaker Groups emerged. Commitment and interest in being a part of the inward and outward journeys of peacemaking are the only requisites for forming a group.

World Peacemakers is funded by tax-deductible contributions.

World Peacemakers, 2852 Ontario Road, N.W., Washington, D.C. 20009. Bill Price, Coordinator. ($1.00)

§

Trick or Treat for UNICEF

This very familiar program had its beginnings in 1950 when one Sunday School class in Pennsylvania collected for UNICEF at Halloween. Later, October 31 became National UNICEF Day by presidential proclamation. It is a day when individuals and groups of all ages participate in the traditional "Trick or Treat for UNICEF" by collecting funds in a variety of ways for the children of the world.

Many churches continue to sponsor "Trick or Treat for UNICEF" with children ringing doorbells and adults coordinating plans. Often a Halloween party is planned for the ingathering of funds. (See page 89 of text.)

The U.S. Committee for UNICEF offers "Trick or Treat for UNICEF" collection cartons, posters, promotional bookmarks, a publicity kit, and several educational leaflets at no charge. The Committee also has information on several other fund-raising programs that have been developed as an outgrowth of "Trick or Treat for UNICEF." These programs include: Shopping Center Collections, a UNICEF Thanksgiving, Auctions and Flea Markets, Matching Funds, Mini-olympics, Read-a-thons, Carnivals, a Haunted House, Sports Events and Tournaments, and Music for UNICEF. Funds received from all of these go to help governments provide supplies, equipment, and long-term services for children in over 100 countries.

UNICEF is nonpolitical. It helps children throughout the world regardless of race, religion, or nationality. It is financed entirely by voluntary contributions from governments and concerned people in more than 120 nations.

U.S. Committee for UNICEF, 331 East 38th Street, New York, New York 10016. Lloyd Bailey, Executive Secretary.

§

Foreign Student Weekend

The text (see page 86) outlines the general format for a Foreign Student Weekend used by churches in McHenry and Oregon, Illinois when Dr. Corbett was pastor.

Capitol Hill United Methodist Church in Washington, D.C. chose the first Sunday in October one year to entertain international students. This is the Sunday when Protestant churches around the globe are celebrating Worldwide Communion Sunday. The students came knowing they would be asked during the worship service to tell briefly about their home churches and their plans for the future. This was done just prior to the communion service with the students seated in a circle within the chancel area. They were served communion while still in the circle to symbolize the fact that people of all races and nationalities would be coming to the Lord's Table that day.

International students coming to the United States under sponsorship of scholarship programs are frequently brought to a campus for a week or two of orientation before their studies begin. Nearby churches are sometimes asked to cooperate by selecting homes where the students can spend a weekend observing American customs and home life. Students thoroughly enjoy sharing in the family shopping, meal preparation, etc. The friendships made are often lasting ones.

J. Elliott Corbett, 100 Maryland Avenue, N.E., Washington, D.C. 20002.

Rural Programs

1. Pike County Outreach Council
2. Emergency and Self-help Housing Programs
3. Migrant Ministry
4. Migrant Ministries of Allen County
5. Rural Mission
6. The North Country Wood Cooperative
7. Missouri Delta Ecumenical Ministry
8. Local Church Outreach

§

Pike County Outreach Council

An ecumenical agency funded by the United Church of Christ, the United Presbyterian Church in the U.S.A., and the United Methodist Church, the Pike County Outreach Council came into being through the vision and efforts of a Presbyterian minister and a Catholic priest. It attempts to be the church, addressing the social, economic, and personal needs of Pike County, which is one of the Appalachian counties in southeastern Ohio.

The 1970 census figures indicated that nearly 43% of the residents of Pike County had not gone beyond the eighth grade in school, and that nearly one-fourth of the families were living on incomes below federal poverty levels. There was a high unemployment rate and a ratio of patients to doctors that was over twice the national average.

The Outreach Council sponsors annually a summer health fair to bring health care information and professional medical people to outlying areas of the county. It has offered a "Reading Is Fundamental" program, field trips, local clubs, and first aid courses. Two community wells were repaired so everyone in the community could have safe drinking water. Emergency assistance meets immediate needs for food, clothing, shelter, utilities, and transportation.

The Council has been involved in low-cost solar energy demonstration projects and hopes to develop a community canning center and a cooperative garden project.

The Pike County Outreach Council employs a full-time director who is assisted by VISTA volunteers recruited to work with the youth and senior citizens.

Many aspects of this outreach program could serve as models for a local church or a group of churches meeting community needs. If interested in a work camp experience, a group might consider going to Pike County. A variety of needs have been met by the work camps sponsored by the Outreach Council.

Pike County Outreach Council, 104 South High Street, Waverly, Ohio 45690. Jay Willer, Director.

§

Emergency and Self-help Housing Programs

The Rural Community Action Ministry (RCAM) serving three counties in Maine (see listing under "Counseling Service and Help Lines" on page 147) has two housing programs that could serve as models for other projects.

The newer of the two is a program of the Housing Committee of RCAM. A trailer was purchased, renovated and furnished to serve as emergency housing. It is available to any family in the area served by the Rural Community Action Ministry in need of emergency housing. The family signs an agreement stating they will pay all fuel and light bills for the duration of their stay and reimburse the Rural Community Action Ministry for any damages caused by them—also they will vacate the trailer at the end of three months. RCAM provides the trailer rent-free. The first two families to need the facility had been burned out of their own trailers. One family stayed nearly three months, the other only three weeks.

Adequate housing is a serious problem in this rural section of Maine. The Housing Committee sponsors a self-help housing program which uses church- and homeowner-donated materials and volunteer labor to improve those homes most in need of repair. During the summer months, local volunteer labor is supplemented with volunteers from churches in New York, New Jersey, and Connecticut.

Rural Community Action Ministry, Franciscan Monastery, Greene, Maine 04236.

Migrant Ministry

For more than 20 years women of Barrington, Illinois have worked to meet the needs of Spanish-speaking people. The channel for this outreach has been the Social (Migrant) Ministry Committee of Church Women United.

First came the truck-farming migrants and their families to harvest the crops. Their stay in Barrington wasn't long each year, but their needs were many. Services and programs had to be created, and the Migrant Ministry Committee rallied the support of the community.

There are few migrants in the Barrington area today. Old housing has been torn down or renovated for the affluent. A few Spanish-speaking families have been helped to "settle in" and are now independent. Others have moved to other communities to find subsidized or older housing.

When the Church Women United of Barrington began their migrant ministry, there were few governmental agencies providing social services. Although the Social (Migrant) Ministry Committee continues to reach out to people, it is seeking new directions for meeting needs. Delegates from 12 churches serve on the Committee.

If you wish to learn about programs that proved effective in working with migrant families, write to:

Social (Migrant) Ministry Committee of the Church Women United of the Barrington Area, c/o Mrs. Daryl Frey, 130 Grace Lane, Barrington, Illinois 60010. (25¢)

§

Migrant Ministries of Allen County

Migrant Ministries of Allen County is a program effort of the Associated Churches of Fort Wayne and Allen County in Indiana to respond to the needs of migrant farmworkers and their families who are housed each summer on the outskirts of Monroeville.

Conditions and difficulties vary from year to year, but Migrant Ministries of Allen County attempts to be flexible in its support. It provides leadership in securing appropriate federal, state, and local programs that will benefit the migrants. Funds and volunteers for these and other programs come from both the Protestant and Catholic churches in the area.

In 1977 Migrant Ministries negotiated a contract with Child Care of Allen County for the administration of a day-care center for migrant children of preschool age. C.C.A.C. organized and operated the center and applied for Title XX funds. Migrant Ministries remained directly involved in making decisions and in providing the matching funds required by Title XX and for other expenses.

A medical program originated some years before by Migrant Ministries was supplanted by a federal program. However, Migrant Ministries stepped in to interpret the new voucher system for emergency care to both hospitals and migrants. Routine health care was provided by Matthew 25 (see page 153) and the Well-Baby Clinic already in existence.

A slide presentation of this ministry was prepared for use of churches.

The Associated Churches, 6430 Upper Huntington Road, Fort Wayne, Indiana 46804. Melvin R. Phillips, Executive Director.

§

Rural Mission

Rural Mission, Inc. is an interdenominational nonprofit organization chartered in 1969 "to foster, promote, and administer to the spiritual, economic, social, educational, medical, and housing requirements of the rural people of South Carolina." It still seeks to find new and effective ways to help the desperately poor of the Sea Islands. Programs it helps to administer include:

—Social services to Island residents.
—A Health Care Center.
—A strong Migrant Ministry to seasonal farm workers.
—A Cultural Arts and Recreational Development program to introduce disadvantaged children to music, arts, and crafts.
—The Esau Jenkins Opportunity Center with facilities for sleeping, recreation, remedial reading classes, etc.
—A Quilting Cooperative.
—A Seafood Cooperative.
—A Mini-farming/Family Gardening Project.

Rural Mission is responsible for seeking funds, finding staff, and overseeing these projects. Rural Mission also sponsors many work camps with volunteers from across the country coming to paint, repair, and construct homes on the Islands.

Rural Mission, Inc., P.O. Box 235, Johns Island, South Carolina 29455 Linda D. Gadson, Administrator; the Reverend Willis T. Goodwin, Founder and Director of Public Relations.

The North Country Wood Cooperative

The urgent need to find alternative fuel sources and a growing concern for the economic welfare of people living in the North Country led the Community Church of Christ in Franconia, New Hampshire in 1978 to organize a wood cooperative. Though several broad goals were established, the primary objective is to provide wood as a supplement to other fuels to reduce the cost of heating homes of low-income families, the elderly, and the handicapped.

The general plan calls for members of the North Country Wood Cooperative to share in the cutting of timber in winter and spring months, hauling and splitting in the summer, and making deliveries by fall. Those unable to participate in the heavy physical labor will be given other responsibilities. Wood will be distributed on the basis of the number of hours worked.

Cooperative members will be selected with the help of community welfare agencies. Policies will be determined by an advisory board composed of 15 members drawn from the church and the Wood Cooperative. Private landowners will donate use of land and the cut wood, and can deduct this contribution from their income tax.

Grants and borrowed equipment were used to get the project off the ground. Some capital will be generated through sale of wood to summer camps, small fees, and contributions to offset the cost of gas, truck rental, and needed equipment. The Community Church of Christ is providing office space, telephone, and land for splitting and storing of wood.

The North Country Wood Cooperative is encouraging other nearby communities to start similar ventures. Equipment could be shared to provide financial savings for all groups.

Thought is also being given to the development of a training program for youth and unemployed adults in logging and woodworking skills.

Community Church of Christ, Franconia, New Hampshire 03580. The Reverend William Briggs.

§

Missouri Delta Ecumenical Ministry

This is an ecumenical ministry working for social and economic development in the Boot-heel of southeastern Missouri, considered one of the most poverty-ridden rural areas in the United States. The basic beliefs of the Missouri Delta Ecumenical Ministry include:

—that the struggle for social justice and human rights is essential to the concept of religion and to the fulfillment of God's plans as revealed in Judaeo-Christian teachings;
—that poor people have the right and necessity to participate more fully in existing political, economic, and social systems;
—the importance of a racially integrated organization and society, in which opportunities are not determined according to race;
—achievement of change through nonviolent means.

To motivate the poor to improve the conditions of their communities, the Missouri Delta Ecumenical Ministry works in four basic fields: social action, youth development, communications, and economic development.

M.D.E.M. has helped to establish or assist neighborhood improvement groups, low-income parent organizations, a legal services program, and welfare rights groups. It has also involved residents in efforts to have utility rates and welfare benefits set at levels which will allow a decent standard of living.

The Youth Development program provides opportunities for low-income young people to develop confidence in themselves. M.D.E.M. conducts job application workshops, information sessions on post-secondary education, and career-planning workshops.

An important part of M.D.E.M.'s ministry is facilitating communications among low-income people seeking to improve conditions, and between these individuals and the officials who make decisions which affect their lives. This is done through a monthly newspaper, community forums, films, and meetings with church leaders, civic groups, and government agencies.

The Missouri Delta Ecumenical Ministry is working to increase the number of good jobs by encouraging the development of small businesses, by attracting new industries to the area, and by securing the maximum number of public employment opportunities. M.D.E.M. provides job training and prepares applicants for interviews and filing of applications.

M.D.E.M. is governed by an interfaith and interracial Board of Directors of 21 persons, the majority of whom come from the low-income community. The ministry is supported by the Roman Catholic Church, six Protestant denominations, the St. Louis Rabbinical Association, private foundations, and concerned individuals and congregations across the country.

Missouri Delta Ecumenical Ministry, P. O. Box 524, Hayti, Missouri 63851. Larry Levine, Executive Director.

§

Local Church Outreach

Members of Los Alamos churches were long ago confronted with the fact that they lived in a community of education and affluence that could be compared to an island set in a sea of poverty and inadequate education in northern New Mexico.

One of the first steps to earn the trust and friendship of the Spanish-speaking people of the rural areas, a prerequisite for having aid accepted, was initiated by the New Mexico Interchurch Agency. Known as HELP (Home Education Livelihood Program), the project prepared individuals for graduation equivalency tests, provided training programs for developing trade skills, and encouraged better health and nutrition with courses in these fields.

(Background information on the growth and current development programs of HELP is available from the HELP State Office, 5000 Marble, N. E., Suite 222, Albuquerque, New Mexico 87110.)

Eloy Martinez, a leader of Centro Campesino de Salud, a rural health organization spawned by HELP, challenged and inspired members of the Christian Social Concerns Work Area of the First United Methodist Church in Los Alamos to become involved in alleviating the suffering and poverty of rural families. First Church members continue to be concerned and committed after more than ten years and include the following in a list of accomplishments:

—Provided funds for a 20-by-20-foot addition to a one-room house that served as the living quarters for a medically disabled man, his wife, and their 14 children. (Four children have since entered college, one graduating with a master's degree.)

—Aided a community of seven families, which had only a polluted well for water, in its struggle to have a pipe laid that would connect the area to a water main. Church members surveyed the water line, took care of legal requirements and worked side-by-side with residents in digging several hundred feet of ditch for the installation of the pipe.

—With the Santa Cruz United Methodist Church, started Project Amigo, a traveling thrift shop of household goods and clothing that had been collected and repaired for distribution. This service had been spun off and is now sponsored by the Immaculate Heart of Mary Catholic Church, which had to drop the traveling aspect but reports buyers coming from a radius of 100 to 150 miles.

—Established a high-risk loan fund from which the pastor of the church can lend money for such emergency needs as purchasing food stamps, paying utility bills, making a rent deposit, helping an ill patient with transportation to a hospital for surgery, etc. (Most of those being helped would be too proud to accept charity.)

- Offered a variety of services as new businesses were being established.
- Purchased a video tape playback unit with monitor for Centro Campesino de Salud to use in its educational efforts in eleven health clinics.
- Assisted with the collecting of more than 1,000 blankets and 3,000 pairs of shoes for distribution by Centro Campesino de Salud.
- Collected usable furniture and appliances and found new homes for them among the rural families.
- Assisted financially with the "Children's Day Out" program of the Los Alamos Family Council. Aged parents are taken and cared for while a son or daughter shops, runs errands, or just gets away for a few hours.
- Sponsor an annual mitten tree at Christmas with mittens going to the needy. This project involves the children of the church.

First United Methodist Church is also participating in an ecumenical project called Self Help, created by the local Lutheran, Roman Catholic, and United Methodist Churches of Los Alamos. Self Help assists low-income individuals in solving their personal needs and problems. In addition to having a paid director, Self Help uses the time and talents of many within the church community. First Church includes funding for the project in its regular church budget.

It might be added that the Christian Concerns Work Area has presented several church-wide studies and workshops for various age groups on subjects that call for moral and ethical judgments to be made from a Christian perspective.

First United Methodist Church, P.O. Box 299 (715 Diamond Drive), Los Alamos, New Mexico 87544. The Reverend David A. Shaw, Pastor.

§

Youth Programs

1. Second Mile House
2. Blue Gargoyle Youth Service Center
3. CYR: Center for Youth Resources
4. Indian Tutorial Program
5. The Special Olympics

§

Second Mile House

Several years ago the First United Methodist Church of Hyattsville, Maryland saw an increasing need for crisis intervention for runaway youth. Its Commission on Social Concerns responded by establishing the Second Mile House, a project which has grown into an interdenominational community effort involving county organizations and services.

Through Second Mile House a Youth Resources Center has been established for adolescents who cannot solve their problems through available community services. Youth are encouraged to call or stop by to discuss their problems. Also, foster-home care is provided with counseling sessions for individuals and families when needed.

Attempts are made to bring about family reconciliation whenever possible. This is achieved through crisis-intervention counseling by trained staff.

Second Mile House, Queens Chapel and Queensbury Roads, Hyattsville, Maryland 20782.

§

Blue Gargoyle Youth Service Center

Begun as a coffee house in 1968 by divinity school student volunteers and University Church (Disciples of Christ), the Blue Gargoyle Youth Service Center in Chicago is now dedicated to meeting the needs of neighborhood youth.

Programs of this nonprofit, community-based agency include tutoring for junior and senior high school students, classes to prepare people for the high school equivalency exam, counseling and assistance in applying for college admission and financial aid, in-service training and counseling on employment, emergency legal services, and workshops led by police officers and attorneys on how the criminal justice system works.

Direction Sports, one of the newer programs, motivates fourth, fifth, and sixth graders to improve basic math and reading skills by making use of sports language and celebrities. A math problem, for instance, may be computing batting averages. Eight high school students and recent graduates serve as the tutor-coaches for the 32 students, who meet four times a week. Parents come once a week to develop new skills that will improve their ability to help their children. Sports celebrities meet personally with both students and parents to emphasize the importance of learning.

The Blue Gargoyle has a food service program that offers a balanced vegetarian meal at a low cost each noon. Over 200 students, faculty, staff, and community residents come to eat lunch in a people-oriented setting. Up to ten youth receive job training each year in the food service and other Gargoyle service programs.

Basketball is one of the main recreational interests at the Gargoyle, with 75 selected each year to participate on teams organized for competition. Stress is placed on discipline, cooperation, and self-expression. Ping-pong and pool are also favorites at the Drop In Center, and "disco" dances attract more than 500.

Programs and services of the Blue Gargoyle Youth Service Center are supported by contributions from church agencies, foundations, businesses, and individuals. University Church donates space, the rental value of which has been estimated at $40,000 annually. There is a paid staff of eight with a board of directors to determine policies.

Blue Gargoyle Youth Service Center, University Church, 5655 South University, Chicago, Illinois 60637. Susan Tobias, Director. (25¢)

§

CYR: Center for Youth Resources

The CYR has quietly fought since 1971 to stem the rising rate of school dropouts, functional illiteracy, and delinquency. It is winning that fight because CYR offers a second chance.

The Center for Youth Resources is one of many projects of Center City Churches, Inc., a coalition of eight downtown churches (Protestant and Catholic) in Hartford, Connecticut. CYR brought together the youth programs of several of these churches with all activities centered in the Central Baptist Church.

The first programs went under the names of *The Opening* and *Coffee House,* reflecting the wish that these be cultural and educational forums for neighborhood youth 13 to 18 years of age. However, it required the lure of athletic events, including basketball, weight lifting, and karate, to attract youngsters from the streets.

The physical programs highlighting staff with their own athletic achievements as role models, began to share the stage with new developments. Lecturers on minority group history, sex education, and drug abuse appeared. Young women enjoyed the classes in good grooming, sewing, and ceramics offered by volunteer instructors. Field trips became popular.

The consciouness raising achieved by the influx of cultural programs paved the way for acceptance of a tutorial program planned to combat low grades, poor attendance, lack of motivation, and rejection of school.

In 1974, the "Stay in School" program was launched. In the first two years more than 500 referrals were made to CYR from the city public schools of youth who had either dropped out of school or were likely to do so. CYR made contact with over 200, persuading them to participate in tutorial programs, attend alternative educational programs, or return to school. A tutorial program is offered each summer to 30 middle school students who would not be promoted if they did not have this extra assistance.

Additional summer programs include dance and drama groups. There is a year-round emphasis on career and higher education counseling.

Center City Churches, Inc., 170 Main Street, Hartford, Connecticut 06106. Ronald Armstrong, CYR Director.

§

Indian Tutorial Program

The First United Methodist Church of Reno, Nevada organized a tutorial program for Indian students several years ago in response to a need highlighted by teachers. A director was selected from the Indian Colony of Reno. Although the first tutors were members of the church, they have been gradually replaced by young adults and high school students from the Indian Colony.

The program, for grades one through high school, continues to attract 35 to 50 students and meets four evenings a week at the church. Each session begins with a light supper or refreshments served by the director and tutors.

A feeling of goodwill and interest has been generated by the program in the church and community, and the public schools report a definite improvement in the grade averages of the Indian students participating.

First United Methodist Church, P.O. Box 789, Reno, Nevada 89504. Contact person: Barbara C. Moore. (15¢)

§

The Special Olympics

For the past several years members of the First United Methodist Church of Reno, Nevada have been actively involved with the Special Olympics for retarded youth of Washoe County.

Church members prepare and serve 150 lunches, serve as timekeepers and scorekeepers, and provide moral support by hugging and congratulating each participant as he or she crosses the finish line.

First United Methodist Church, P.O. Box 789, Reno, Nevada 89504. Contact person: Barbara C. Moore (15¢)

§

APPENDIX

APPENDIX

A MODERN PARAPHRASE OF THE LETTER OF JAMES

A Prophet of Action

Count it all joy, my brethren, when you meet various trials, for you know that the testing of your faith produces steadfastness. (1:2-3)
For when you are ill, you will better appreciate the One who makes you whole,
And when you are unjustly criticized, you will speak a good word for God.
And when all people persecute you, One Being shall hold you up.
Be doers of the word, and not hearers only. (1:22)
Feel the grace of a merciful God,
    and forgive those who offend you.
Listen to my warnings about the rich
    and give generously to the poor.
Hear the cries of the hurt: the pained in body, the tormented in soul, the faint in heart, and serve their many needs.
If you think more highly of those who drive expensive cars to church and park them conspicuously near the door, and poke fun at those who arrive on bicycles, then you deceive yourselves.
Is your $10-a-week giver treated with more respect that the honestly poor person who gives of her widow's mite?
Do you mostly select successful businessmen for your ushering duties?
Is there anyone who passes the plate in the pew to whom the just church should offer its contents?
Are the poor uncomfortable in your midst?
Are people entitled to respect by the way they dress on Sunday or the way they earn their living during the week?
My brethren, show no partiality as you hold the faith. (2:1)

Persons are persons. If you favor those who have good jobs, are successful, the leaders of the church, the financial pillars of the congregation, you are transgressors. Seek out the poor for your attention, greet the unknown visitor, embrace the powerless retired couple, be warm toward your minority members, make the grouch smile.

What does it profit, my brethren, if a man says he has faith but has not works? Can his faith save him? (2:14)

There is little point in our saying to the hungry of the world: have faith, read the Scriptures, pray—when their bellies are distended with starvation. Show your faith by feeding them. Then maybe they can think about spiritual matters and get their minds off their next meal. The Word of God becomes flesh when you show you care about those who are all skin and bones. Do not be so cruel as to merely hand them the Scriptures. Do you want them to eat paper along with the bark they gnaw off young trees?

Faith and works are inseparably intertwined. No one can say, "I am strong in faith but you are strong in works."

Faith is the sturdy plant with deep roots; works are the flowers. If you cut off the flower, it could grow again. If you destroy the roots, you have destroyed the flower as well. But there are some rosebushes that produce no roses, while other rosebushes are fertilized and produce many flowers. Roots and roses, faith and works; they belong together. Let your faith be nourished in the firm ground of Scripture and prayer; let your works grow naturally from your faith, offering a witness of beauty.

The tongue is an unrighteous world among our members, staining the whole body. (3:6)

Do not be busybodies, but let your bodies be busy in the Lord's work.

Be restrained in what you say. Do not be boastful; if you have excelled, let others tell of it. And do not gossip, glorying in the misfortune of others. All persons make mistakes, but don't dwell on them. Make sure you know what you are talking about—and then don't talk. If you know something good about someone, spread it around. If you know something bad about someone, hold your tongue with your hand. Do not make yourself tall by stepping on the bodies of others. Remember that your stature will depend on who you are and what you do. When you cut down other people, you dwarf yourself.

Where jealousy and selfish ambition exist, there will be disorder and every vile practice. (3:16)

For if you despise others because they excel or hate them because they stand in the way of your own achievement, you will come to naught. For you will speak evil of others and elbow them aside to win the race.

You will end up ashamed of what you do, and slow your progress by carrying guilt toward your goal.

Be a human being. Exult in the good success of others, as though they were your own children. Take pride in the recognition of your friends, for they are a part of you.

Let the spiritual wisdom from above be your guide. Let no man or woman be your enemy or your competitor for acclaim. Deal gently with all, giving them the benefit of the doubt and all praise for what you are sure of about them. Learn to live peacefully with all persons, accepting their just criticisms, absorbing their blows, forgiving their unforgivable actions, because you know God and understand why people act the way they do.

What causes wars, and what causes fightings among you? Is it not your passions that are at war in your members? You desire and do not have; so you kill. And you covet and cannot obtain; so you fight and wage war. (4:1-2)

Would you go to war over oil in the Middle East?

Do you want the United States to stake out the resources on the ocean floor even at the risk of war?

Do you so desire the copper of Zaire that you are willing to arm her to the teeth in an extremely explosive situation?

Do you covet both Arab oil and the American Jewish vote enough to sell weapons to both sides in the Middle East?

Was your anti-communist passion so great that you were willing to help depose a leftist Chilean government, even if it meant the emergence of a military regime that would be at war with its own citizens?

Was your passion so blind that your leaders were willing to attempt an assassination of Castro even if such a venture might threaten the life of an American president?

§

Draw near to God in the morning.
Draw near to God in the evening.
Draw near to God in the tumult.
Draw near to God in the calm.
Draw near to God among close friends.
Draw near to God when alone.
Draw near to God when victorious.
Draw near to God in defeat.
Draw near to God and he will draw near to you. (4:8)

§

Humble yourselves before the Lord and he will exalt you. (4:10)
Admit your dependence upon God, and he will hold you up.
Acknowledge the Lord's mighty works, and he will help you do good.
Glorify the power of God Almighty, and he will convert your weakness into strength.
Come now, you rich, weep and howl for the miseries that are coming upon you. . . . You have laid up treasure for the last days (5:1,3),
For your wealth will do you no good,
If in your last days you are too feeble to travel to faraway places,
Too ill to eat gourmet food,
Too misshapen to fit tailored clothes,
And too senile to spend your ill-gotten gain.
You have lived on the earth in luxury and in pleasure (5:5),
And turned away from the sight of those in distress.
Therefore, the "no vacancy" sign will be hung out in my Father's mansion,
And you will stand aside while the poor are registered.
You have fattened your hearts in a day of slaughter (5:5),
Clipping coupons and receiving dividends on profits made from weapons production,
Satisfied to cleanse blood money by giving pennies to the church out of the riches acquired from war gain.
But above all. . . do not swear. (5:12)
Let your language be simple, and do not use God's name to prove you are telling the truth.
Say simply "Yes" or "No" for you need not involve the deity in order to verify your integrity,
For persons will believe your word as they learn to trust it.
The prayer of a righteous man has great power in its effects. (5:16)
And so, try to be righteous,
For those who can best stand before God can best bow before him.
Be ministers of grace in all your good works.
And when you intercede with God in supplication, he will send his power flowing through your spirit,
And the sick will be healed, the sojourner protected, and the troubled will find peace.

NOTES

1. Albert Henry Newman, *A Manual of Church History* (Valley Forge, PA: Judson Press, 1933), p. 607.
2. Courtesy of Clayton Fritchey.
3. *Situation Ethics* (Philadelphia: Westminster Press, 1966), p. 87, Fletcher's italics.
4. Kenneth Thompson, *Christian Ethics and the Dilemmas of Foreign Policy* (Durham, NC: Duke University Press, 1959), pp. 83-86.
5. (Washington, D.C.: Board of Christian Social Concerns, 1961), p. 21.
6. Louis D. Brandeis, *Other People's Money* (New York: Frederick A. Stokes Company, 1932), p. 92.
7. This is a free translation from the Greek, as it appears on the masthead of the Friends Committee on National Legislation *Newsletter.*
8. *Decision-Making in World Affairs,* p. 21.
9. As quoted in John C. Bennett, *Christians and the State* (New York: Charles Scribner's Sons, 1958), pp. 288-289.
10. Roswell P. Barnes, *Under Orders: The Church and Public Affairs* (New York: Doubleday, 1961), pp. 87-88.
11. Information for the section on World Hunger was taken from *Meeting Basic Human Needs: The U.S. Stake in a New Developmental Strategy,* a report of the 25th Anniversary International Development Conference; February 7-9, 1978; Washington, D.C.
12. Leesburg, VA: WMSE Publications, p. 6.
13. *SALT II: Toward a More Secure World,* U.S. Arms Control and Disarmament Agency; Washington, D.C.; 1979.
14. This quotation appears in *More Jobs,* a pamphlet produced by the Coalition for a New Foreign and Military Policy.
15. *Basic Facts About UNICEF,* U.S. Committee for UNICEF, New York, 1979.
16. This quotation appeared in the "Human Rights Day Observance" brochure, United Nations Association, Washington, D.C., December 10, 1979. For a copy of the Human Rights Day observance of the United Nations Association in Washington, write to Ms. Sophie Degan, Capital Area Division, U.N.A.—U.S.A., 3141 N Street, N.W., Washington, D.C. 20007.
17. Contents of the box are referred to in various letters, dated between August 30 and September 20, 1962, in files of the Division of World Peace, Board of Church and Society of The United Methodist Church, Washington, D.C.